PRAISE FOR

3 HOURS A DAY

As a serial entrepreneur I have launched many businesses and I know firsthand how overwhelming launching and running a successful enterprise can be. Knolly Williams is continually giving his time and expertise to help others become the best version of themselves. In *3 Hours a Day* Knolly lays out a path that any business owner can follow to both streamline and systematize their operation through the intelligent use of leverage.

—**Glenn Sanford,** founder and CEO of eXp Realty

Entrepreneurship doesn't have to be a grind. Follow the success clues offered by Knolly Williams to live the lifestyle you dreamed of when setting out on your entrepreneurial journey. His proven strategies and tactics are just what you need TODAY to succeed now and into the future.

—**Tom Hopkins,** author of *How to Master the Art of Selling* and chairman and founder of the renowned sales training organization, Tom Hopkins International

Knolly teaches extremely important tools to thrive, not just survive, in business. *3 Hours a Day* outlines tangible steps to integrate transformative concepts into your life and business, so you have more time to enjoy what you've built.

—**Anne Mahlum,** founder and chairperson of Solidcore and CEO of Ambition

Knolly has written a masterpiece of not just business but life planning: a simple step-by-step road map to productivity and success focused on measuring results and not just the effort that goes into them. This is a must-read for every entrepreneur or those aspiring to be one.

—**Josh Cadillac,** author of *Close for Life: The Real Estate Agent's Guide to Creating Satisfied Customers that Only Do Business with You*

I've been a producer for the *Today Show* and have been privileged to work alongside Mel Robbins, Grant Cardone, and many others when they were first introduced to the world. Knolly has that rare quality of greatness, and the ideas he hits on in this new book are perfectly timed for today's entrepreneurial revolution. Knolly has the power to transform lives, and I'm positive your life will be forever touched by this amazing book.

    —Hank Norman, the "Modern-Day Media Mogul," brand builder, coach, and entrepreneur

3 Hours a Day is a must-read if you want to maximize your productivity and achieve your goals . . . faster. Priority management is an old subject, but Knolly Williams's approach is fresh and very today. Knolly's insights are based on years of experience and research, and he presents them in a clear, concise, and engaging manner that makes it easy to apply his strategies in your own life. This book is filled with practical advice and actionable steps for utilizing the power of focus, discipline, and purpose to make the most of just "3 Hours a Day."

    —Don Hobbs, former president of Jim Rohn Productions, former president of *Success* magazine, cofounder of Expert Partners and Hobbs/Herder, and one of the top 25 most influential people in real estate, according to *Realtor* magazine

I have worked with many of the greatest entrepreneurs in the industry, and Knolly stands out for me as one of the greats. He is a likable and talented thought leader who deserves to be heard. *3 Hours a Day* is BIG IDEA, and Knolly has written a true gem of a book.

    —Steve Carlis, winner of the Ernst and Young Entrepreneur of the Year Award (2000), founder of 2 Market Media, and executive producer of more than 50 films, including the Academy Award–nominated *Sling Blade*

Knolly has done what millions of people dream of doing, all while keeping his faith number one in his life. Not only has he lived the "3 Hours a Day" blueprint, he has broken it down in a way that others can understand and apply to live their own dream life. This book will show you what true success looks like.

    —Nicholas Bayerle, CEO of The King's Brotherhood and bestselling author of *The Modern Day Business Man*

I've watched Knolly Williams for over a decade (up close and in person) live the "3 Hours a Day" lifestyle. He doesn't just teach it—he actually lives it! He is abundantly wealthy in all areas of his life: his life is full of memorable experiences, rich relationships, and finances.
  —**Fred Weaver,** Cofounder of Group 46:10

This book is a guide that shatters the conventional wisdom of 'working harder' by offering real strategies for achieving financial success and personal fulfillment while working less. Knolly masterfully combines research, real-life stories, and a step-by-step guide to streamlining processes and prioritizing tasks. By embracing the "3 Hours a Day" philosophy, entrepreneurs can break free from the shackles of endless work, boosting their productivity, creativity, and more importantly, happiness.
  —**Tristan Ahumada,** chief marketing officer of *Success* magazine, Fortune 500 consultant, international speaker, and director of Lab Coat Agents, the largest real estate Facebook Group in the world

If you're looking for a practical and inspiring guide to achieving success in real estate, *3 Hours A Day* is a must-read. What sets this book apart is its emphasis on efficiency and productivity: Knolly will show you how to maximize your time and efforts to generate more leads, close more deals, and ultimately, earn more money, providing clear and actionable advice on everything from leadership, business growth, negotiation, time management, and mindset. *3 Hours A Day* is more than a how-to guide. It's a book that motivates and empowers readers to take control of their lives and create the financial freedom they desire.
  —**Kevin Kauffman,** Cofounder of Group 46:10

I have had the privilege to get to know Knolly Williams over the years and I can tell you he's the real deal. I have coached tens of thousands of entrepreneurs and real estate agents, and I am constantly looking for fresh and new angles to help them become more productive and successful. Knolly's new book, *3 Hours a Day*, checks both boxes. It contains a systematic method for working smarter, and I highly recommend it if you are interested in scaling your business hassle-free!
  —**Jay Kinder,** coauthor of *Miracle Morning for Real Estate Agents* and one of *Realtor* magazine's Top 30 under 30 (2003)

Knolly's ideas and approach to entrepreneurship are unique and refreshing. I am blown away by his breadth of knowledge, and I am confident that your life and business will be incredibly impacted by this amazing book.

—**Cliff Freeman,** CEO of the Mega eXpansion Group at eXp
Realty and a highly sought-after real estate coach and trainer

My man Knolly Williams is a true inspiration to so many entrepreneurs! I really love his style and his heart to help others be their best. In his book *3 Hours a Day,* Knolly lays out a plan that will empower you to live a life that is rich and full. You will not only be able to spend more time doing what you love to do, but you'll be working more efficiently and making more money as a result. I highly recommend *3 Hours a Day* to every entrepreneur looking to earn more while working less.

—**Kevin Anson,** celebrity video guru and founder of Ads of Fire

I have had Knolly Williams speak at several of my events to packed rooms, and he always delivers! Our attendees LOVE his content, and I have personally watched him practice what he preaches. In *3 Hours a Day,* Knolly lays out a blueprint for entrepreneurs to finally live the life of FREEDOM they want and deserve. Knolly is a man who follows hard after God and is a light for those seeking to elevate their GAME. If you own a business, you need this book!

—**Brent Gove,** author of *Momentum,* the definitive resource on
how to become a super-agent

I highly recommend *3 Hours a Day* to anyone who wants to achieve financial abundance and time freedom without sacrificing their ethics, morals, or quality of life. Knolly Williams embodies what it means to be successful, and his dedication to living a beautiful life while achieving financial abundance is something that I find inspiring, and it's clear that he is passionate about helping others achieve the same. This book is a valuable resource for anyone who desires to follow in his footsteps.

—**Michael Reese,** coauthor of *Miracle Morning for Real Estate
Agents* and the founder of Life By Strategy

3 HOURS A DAY

How Entrepreneurs
Can Multiply Their
Income by **Working Less**
and **Living More**

KNOLLY WILLIAMS

The Business Healer

Mc
Graw
Hill

New York Chicago San Francisco Athens London Madrid
Mexico City Milan New Delhi Singapore Sydney Toronto

1 2 3 4 5 6 7 8 9   LCR   28 27 26 25 24 23

ISBN   978-1-265-08694-7
MHID   1-265-08694-X

e-ISBN   978-1-265-09028-9
e-MHID   1-265-09028-9

Library of Congress Cataloging-in-Publication Data

Names: Williams, Knolly, author.
Title: 3 Hours a Day : how entrepreneurs can multiply their income by working less and living more / Knolly Williams.
Other titles: Three hours a day
Description: New York : McGraw Hill, [2024] | Includes bibliographical references.
Identifiers: LCCN 2023006959 (print) | LCCN 2023006960 (ebook) | ISBN 9781265086947 (hardback) | ISBN 9781265090289 (ebook)
Subjects: LCSH: Strategic planning. | Work-life balance. | New business enterprises—Management. | Success in business.
Classification: LCC HD30.28 .W546 2024 (print) | LCC HD30.28 (ebook) | DDC 658.4/012—dc23/eng/20230222
LC record available at https://lccn.loc.gov/2023006959
LC ebook record available at https://lccn.loc.gov/2023006960

McGraw Hill books are available at special quantity discounts to use as premiums and sales promotions or for use in corporate training programs. To contact a representative, please visit the Contact Us pages at www.mhprofessional.com.

McGraw Hill is committed to making our products accessible to all learners. To learn more about the available support and accommodations we offer, please contact us at accessibility@mheducation.com. We also participate in the Access Text Network (www.accesstext.org), and ATN members may submit requests through ATN.

This book is dedicated to all of the members of my Mentorship Masters real estate group at eXp Realty and the members of my Knolly Coaching Club entrepreneurs' group. You have been a true source of inspiration for me and have helped me perfect my coaching and training craft. You have made it possible for me to live life by design and experience ultimate time, location, and financial freedom. This book was created to help you become all that God created you to be, so that you can live the life you were meant to live.

CONTENTS

Introduction   vii

CHAPTER 1
Started from the Bottom, and Now I'm Here   1

CHAPTER 2
Embracing 3 Hours a Day   13

CHAPTER 3
Step 1: Hone Your Superpower   29

CHAPTER 4
Step 2: Evaluate Your Business   49

CHAPTER 5
Step 3: Balance Your Business   63

CHAPTER 6
Step 4: Delegate Your Business   77

CHAPTER 7
Step 5: Systematize Your Business   97

CHAPTER 8
Step 6: Design Your 3 Hours a Day   107

CHAPTER 9
Step 7: Quadruple Your Income with 3 Hours a Day   127

CONTENTS

CHAPTER 10
Overcoming the Challenges of 3 Hours a Day   141

CHAPTER 11
Frequently Asked Questions About 3 Hours a Day   153

Acknowledgements   167

Resources   169

Index   173

INTRODUCTION

How would you like to earn six or seven figures a year while working far less and doing what you love to do? How about having nights and weekends off, and as many vacations as you choose? How does being financially free, having the lifestyle you've always dreamed of, the freedom to be able to work from anywhere in the world, and getting it all by working just 3 Hours a Day sound? I bet it sounds good. I also bet you think it's impossible.

On the face of it, working only three hours in a day sounds ridiculous. How is it possible to get everything you need done in three hours, when you can scarcely get it all done in 8 or 10 hours? It probably hasn't even crossed your mind that you could work three hours a day and be just as productive, if not more so, than in a full work day. You may think to yourself, I wish there was an easier way. I wish there was a way to be able to choose more for my life. As a young entrepreneur I had the same thoughts, but over the past forty years of my entrepreneurial journey, I discovered a smarter way. For more than a decade, I have had the freedom to work wherever I want, whenever I want . . . and I have taught thousands of entrepreneurs how to do the same.

I'm here to tell you that this book contains **the way**.

My name is Knolly Williams, and I'm called the Business Healer. The life I live daily is a life that many entrepreneurs dream of, but don't know how to get to in a practical way. In this book, I bring you the system that many of my coaching clients have paid tens of thousands of dollars to learn. I will help you demystify the process and break down exactly how you can quadruple your income while working just 3 Hours a Day—as you'll see it referred to throughout this book.

ARE YOU LIVING BY DESIGN OR BY DEFAULT?

If you had told me back when I was 23 that there was a way for me to earn a lot more money doing what I loved to do, all while working just three hours each day, I would have looked you in the eye and told you that you were crazy. Before I began living my life by design, I never would have believed it was possible, either.

Maybe you believe that you don't have a choice over the life you're living, that your only choice is to work long hours in order to be successful, that missing out on your kids growing up or putting less time into your relationship with your spouse because you're working so much to provide for them is the only way. Or, maybe you believe that putting your health on the back burner is just the way it has to be in order to get everything you want. That's called "default living," and it's costing you the most important things in life. Living by default is allowing life to happen to you, instead of *you* orchestrating the life you choose to experience. Most people live by default because they simply don't realize that there is another, more empowered way to live.

Ironically, living life by default will also ultimately cost you financially. While you may think that working more is going to get you more money, you will most assuredly net far less in the long run. There are three primary reasons why working more could wind up netting you far less:

1. **Lost years of productivity.** What I have learned after working with tens of thousands of entrepreneurs is that burning the candle at both ends inevitably leads to burnout, which can cost you many years of potential productivity.
2. **Lost opportunities.** When you are working all the time, there is a huge potential to fall into a rut and miss out on new opportunities. When implemented correctly, 3 Hours a Day can keep your mind fast and fresh, teaming with new ideas that lead to increased daily productivity and revenue.
3. **Lost mindshare.** Like your computer hard drive, your brain has storage capacity limitations. As such, I have found that it is best to work on the million-dollar ideas, and leave the thousand-dollar ideas to others.

By working more hours to get more money, you are ultimately falling back into the old employee paradigm of trading time for dollars. The most common mistake made by business leaders and entrepreneurs is measuring their success against the hours they put into their careers. Your success relies on your ability to systemize, organize, automate, and delegate tasks in order to stay *out* of the weeds and focus on growing your business.

This book is going to help you start living and working by design. When you are living in the weeds, you are not able to see through them to the big picture. You have to design the path to get out of where you are and onto major success. As the Business Healer, I have developed a methodology to get you to the ultimate goal: working just 3 Hours a Day, by focusing on only two Big Picture Priorities and delegating all else. This book contains the solution for going from working *in* your business to working *on* your business. When you work on your business instead of working in it, you pull back the weeds (the daily grind) and are able to focus on getting to the big picture success that you deserve.

WHY 3 HOURS A DAY?

I want you to imagine for a moment that you are stuck inside of a maze. As you are making your way through it, you have to decide at each juncture whether you should go right or left. How can you possibly know which way to turn as you make each and every decision? Each possibility along the path could be moving you further away from the exit. Some entrepreneurs spend years going around in circles, trapped inside a maze of their own devising without ever significantly moving the needle toward their success or creating any sense of freedom.

Now, imagine that you have a drone that gives you a bird's-eye view of the maze. 3 Hours a Day is that drone. It allows you to look down on your business and orchestrate the players (your team members) who are left to navigate the labyrinth below. From your vantage point, you can easily direct their steps. You are no longer working *in* your business, but working *on* it.

As a young workaholic entrepreneur, I spent many years working 12 to 16 hours each day, but I knew there had to be a better way. I also knew that I was doing far too many tasks, which I should have been delegating. As I became a master of systems and efficiency, and began training and coaching thousands of fellow entrepreneurs, I noticed many patterns and similarities in my clients' work. I learned to determine exactly what my clients needed to do versus what tasks could be delegated. I found that there were really only two Big Picture Priorities that my clients needed to focus on and that all other tasks could be delegated to someone else. Later, I learned that studies show that humans are only productive on a task for a maximum of 90 minutes.* Thus, 3 Hours a Day was born. This system gives you up to 90 minutes per priority to complete each of the Big Picture Priorities.

I know this 3 Hours a Day system to be true because I am living proof. I spent my twenties working endless hours and making a lot less than I make now on only 3 Hours a Day. In my thirties, I crushed it in the real estate game, where I learned to become a master at leverage. I reached a point where I was working just a few hours a week and earning in the high six-figures. In my forties, I began training, coaching, and paying it forward by teaching and sharing everything I had learned. By the age of 45, I paid off my house and became semiretired, traveling the world and enjoying tons of life experiences and leisure.

I've been living the 3 Hours a Day lifestyle for the past seven years, and in that time, I've run three successful businesses that each make six-plus figures. I am living my dream life, one in which I travel for pleasure 50 percent of my time. (In the last six months alone my wife and I have taken six vacations, including to Puerto Rico; San Diego; Los Cabos, Mexico; and Sarasota, Florida.) Just recently, my wife and I planned a trip to Bali, and we are planning return trips to Spain and Italy. In fact, on our recent trip to Puerto Rico, my wife and I went out looking at homes for sale, just for grins. We made an offer on the second home we saw and moved in about 60 days after our offer was accepted. Our new backyard overlooks the ocean on one side and the mountains on the other.

---

* Wanda Thibodeaux, "Why Working in 90-Minute Intervals Is Powerful for Your Body and Job, According to Science," *Inc.com*, January 27, 2017, https://www.inc.com/wanda-thibodeaux/why-working-in-90-minute-intervals-is-powerful-for-your-body-and-job-according-t.html.

I run a successful YouTube channel with thousands of subscribers and have been featured on major media outlets like CBS, NBC, ABC, and *Newsweek*. I get to speak all over the country; I am featured weekly on various podcasts; and I have a team of leaders and administrators who oversee, manage, and run my operations. I also have a team of more than 300 agents (that will soon grow to more than 1,000) that sell under me in my real estate business and other ventures. In this book, I'll show you step-by-step how you can duplicate and surpass my success no matter your field of expertise.

THE SEVEN-STEP PROCESS

The roadmap for the 3 Hours a Day solution is a step-by-step process that must be followed in sequence. I've coached tens of thousands of entrepreneurs and even taught this information in my 3 Hours a Day bootcamps, so I know for a fact that this process will rejuvenate your life and revolutionize your business, should you choose to implement it. You will unlock windows of time in your daily schedule that you never imagined could exist. You will also free yourself up to work on your terms, while also increasing your net wealth. We will delve into each step in detail later on in the book, but let's take a sneak peek at the seven steps to 3 Hours a Day.

STEP 1: HONE YOUR SUPERPOWER

The first step to 3 Hours a Day is to *hone your superpower*. From my years of study and observation, I can emphatically assure you that you are uniquely wired. You have a unique set of gifts that

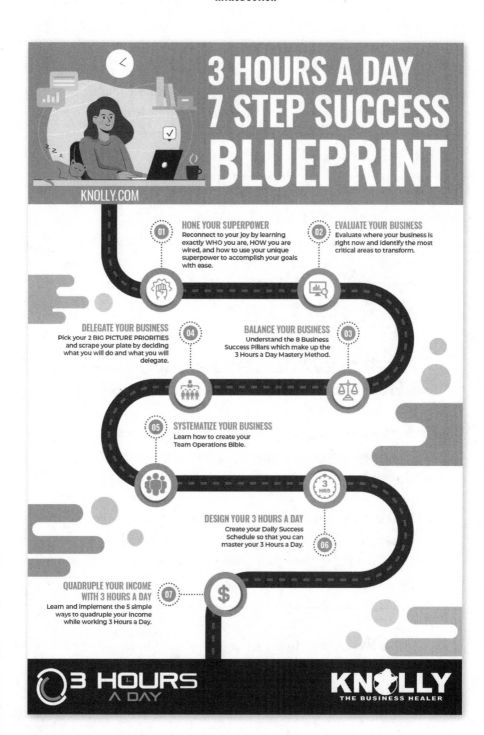

enable you to do certain things much easier than others. For example, I'm really good at connecting with people at an emotional and spiritual level. It's not something that I made up or that I conjured; I came onto the planet with it. Ironically, connecting with others has also been my biggest fear over the years. But once I unlocked that gift, I unlocked success.

Therefore, it is paramount to your success that you figure out your superpower. Here, I will provide you with some techniques to help you discover and understand it so that you can do more of what you are good at and fewer tasks that fall outside of your zone of genius. I will show you how to utilize your unique superpower to create the best experiences possible as you move toward the accomplishment of your ultimate goals.

STEP 2: EVALUATE YOUR BUSINESS: THE FIVE AREAS OF YOUR BUSINESS

Once you have discovered exactly who you are, what you are, and why you are here, it's time to take a good look at where you are in your business, so that you can see exactly which areas need the most immediate attention. Evaluating your business begins with taking a good look at the five critical areas of your business: marketing, sales, delivery, operations, and finance. During this step, the first thing we will do is take a candid look at each area. We will tag it as RED, YELLOW, or GREEN:

RED = I have to do it all.

YELLOW = A few things are working, but I have to keep jumping back in and putting out fires.

GREEN = Everything is dialed in and I can manage it by looking at a number.

While we are at it, I also want you to take a good look at your life. There are 14 areas on the Life Abundance Wheel that make you whole, and your career/business is just one of the 14. The 14 areas are:

1. Physical Environment
2. Adventure and Fun
3. Career and Business
4. Lifestyle
5. Friends and Relationships
6. Finances
7. Giving Back
8. Personal Development
9. Family
10. Travel and Vacations
11. Health and Wellness
12. Happiness
13. Marriage and Intimacy
14. Spirituality

STEP 3: BALANCE YOUR BUSINESS

After evaluating the five primary areas of your business, it's time to move onto balance. To do this, I have created a system that looks at the eight different pillars of your business: mindset, activities, people, systems, tools, money, accountability, and training. It's a holistic approach that will look at both your life and your business, since in many ways the two are inseparable. Once you have a solid understanding of these pillars, you can see exactly where your business needs balance.

Small Business Opportunities magazine actually taught me a lot about franchises. While roughly 80 percent of mom-and-pop restaurants close their doors before hitting the five-year mark, the failure rate for established franchises is less than half that percentage.* In fact, 90 to 95 percent of franchises are profitable.† So why does Jack's Chicken Shack only have a 20 percent chance of succeeding, while those who purchase a Chick-Fil-A franchise enjoy a 95 percent success rate? I discovered that the most successful franchise models all have the eight pillars in place. Franchising helps develop your *mindset* for success in the brand and tells you exactly what *activities* you need to do to build that success. You'll hire the right *people* and implement the *systems* and tools you need for the franchise to succeed. Buying into a franchise requires you to track your *money* and provide *accountability* and *training*. While I'm not advocating for you go out and buy a franchise, the eight pillars will allow you to run your business more like a franchise and reap similar rewards.

STEP 4: DELEGATE YOUR BUSINESS

Now we come to the scariest part of the journey to 3 Hours a Day: it's time to scrape your plate and delegate!

Yes, you will be handing over most of what you do to someone else, but don't freak out; I'll guide you every step of the way. Most entrepreneurs that come to me for coaching have failed miserably in this area. Initially, most of them don't think that delegation works, because they themselves are terrible managers

---

* Jarrett Bellini, "The No. 1 thing to consider before opening a restaurant," *CNBC.com*, March 15, 2016,https://www.cnbc.com/2016/01/20/heres-the-real -reason-why-most-restaurants-fail.html.

† Mark Scott, "The real independent vs. franchise business failure rates," *LinkedIn*, September 1, 2021, https://www.linkedin.com/pulse/real-independent -vs-franchise-business-failure-rates-mark-scott/.

and ineffective leaders when it comes to delegating work. While you may think that you have hired the wrong people in the past, the real issue typically boomerangs back to your leadership style, personal and emotional blocks, and self-limiting beliefs. Once you bring balance to your emotional issues, you can begin to put together a really good team, or repurpose the team you already have.

During this step, I will teach you a simple, bulletproof system for hiring. You will learn WHO to hire and HOW to hire, plus you'll learn my system for getting what I call "leveraged labor." It sounds weird I know, but trust me. It's amazing.

STEP 5: ORGANIZE YOUR BUSINESS

This is the step where you work on creating your Team Operations Bible (TOB). You will take each task in your business and convert it into a one-page standard operating procedure (SOP) document. For example, in my real estate practice I have 46 tasks, which means I have 46 SOPs.

I can feel your eyes glazing over already. Don't worry! Your first hire will actually draft this document for you, using my easy-to-follow instructions.

We will also group each of your activities by what kind of personality is best suited for each task. You will find that some of the tasks will be more administrative in nature, not consumer-facing, while others will be better suited for someone who is great at connecting with people. You will then categorize the tasks and hire someone who encompasses the strengths needed for the position. I'll help you identify the profiles to look for in certain hires and even provide you a job description template, which you can tweak for your specific needs.

Essentially, I will help you get to a place where your business runs efficiently with or without you. You might be able to get there in less than a year. For others, it'll take one or two years, but that's OK, considering that most entrepreneurs don't achieve this level of freedom in their lifetime. Your Team Operations Bible is a key component to making this happen.

STEP 6: DESIGN YOUR 3 HOURS A DAY

Now that you have the help you need and you have an amazing Team Operations Bible in place, you will want to design exactly what your workday is going to look like. In this step, I'll also cover "lead generation." You will learn that there are just three primary lead buckets, from which all the leads you ever need for your business will come: (1) your sphere of influence (SOI/ word of mouth), (2) your farm (a specific geographic or digital area), and (3) your niche (your specificity). Mastering the art of lead generation is essential to your ability to generate consistent cash flow, so here we will cover the four-step lead lifecycle (your funnel): how to generate, capture, incubate, and convert each lead so that none of your future customers or clients will ever fall through the cracks. Remember, *the fortune is in the follow-up*.

It's fun to work all the time when you're first starting something, but eventually, you want to take control of your business instead of having it control you. Do you want to work from nine to noon, or do you want to break up your workday into two 90-minute shifts? It's completely up to you.

This step might be challenging at first, as it seems counter-intuitive to have a fixed schedule as an entrepreneur. But in the case of 3 Hours a Day, you are living by design to become the master of your time!

STEP 7: QUADRUPLE YOUR INCOME

The final step on the seven-step roadmap of 3 Hours a Day is to *quadruple your income*. It seems implausible to purposely cut back on the hours you work each day in order to increase your income, but in this last step I will walk you through five ways that you are going to quadruple your income while working only 3 Hours a Day. By far, the number one way to quadruple your income is through leverage. Scraping your plate of 90 percent of the things that you used to do affords you the freedom to work *on* your business instead of *in* your business, and it allows your business to become as big as *it* wants to be.

• • •

Getting your business to run on 3 Hours a Day is a process, not a single event. This book will serve as your reference guide, a step-by-step manual to assist you as you tread the path toward your ultimate goal. I will provide resources throughout the book that will help you along your journey. You can find a complete list of them at the back of this book and online in downloadable format at 3HoursADay.com/bookresources.

Follow the simple process I lay out in this book to system-ize and organize your business, and not only will you run a far more efficient operation, you will also change your life. You will be living your purpose, perhaps for the first time ever, while only working in the areas of your business that you absolutely love. My system will help you focus only on the things that are important and to delegate all else, making you a more capable and effective leader.

But more than anything else, this book is about freedom—financial freedom, time freedom, and location freedom. You'll learn to prioritize the two big tasks that will move your company forward, working only on the most "income-producing activities" while delegating all of the "non-income-producing activities" to your capable crew. As a leader, your value isn't in putting out small fires. It's in the inspiration and motivation of your team to operate at their peak potential.

CHAPTER 1

Started from the Bottom, and Now I'm Here

ENTREPRENEUR AT TWELVE

Before we deep dive into the precise system that will take you to 3 Hours a Day, I want to share with you my own personal story and what motivates me to help entrepreneurs succeed at their highest potential possible.

The entrepreneurial bug first bit me when I was about twelve years old. Although my mom and dad separated when I was about six, I spent most of my summers with Dad, who was a lifelong entrepreneur. Mom was a social worker and Dad was a salesman and a hustler, and he definitely had game.

I learned later in life that when he was very young, he used to climb the mango trees in Trinidad to pick the sweetest and ripest mangoes to sell at school. Every day he would climb the mango trees in his area, filling his bag with the tasty treats. He was willing to climb high up into the trees and risk his own safety just to pick the best mangoes, which he could charge more for. Since most of the other kids were not willing to risk their necks in this way, Dad was able to build a lucrative business: all the kids and neighborhood folk knew where to go to get the best supply. Eventually, he earned the nickname, Mango Frog.

When my dad turned 18, he decided to move to the United States. When he got here, all he saw was opportunity. In fact, Dad saw opportunity in almost everything. He joined the military so that the government would pay for his college degree. A musician from a young age, he formed his own soul cover band and rounded up the best players he could find, booking gigs all over the Midwest.

In his thirties, he discovered swap meets and flea markets and began selling goods of all kinds. I would tag along as his helper and was able to watch Dad as he worked with his customers. He was suave and silver-tongued. Almost anyone who interacted with him was compelled to purchase something.

I often wonder, Are entrepreneurs just born or are we nurtured and created over time? I suspect it's a little bit of both. I watched my mother go to work every single day, having to be there at a specific time, clock her hours, and be accountable to *the system*. While she made really good money, that path seemed far too constricting to me. Meanwhile, my father woke up when he wanted to and went to work whenever he wanted to (mostly when his funds were low). Although he was no financial wizard, he seemed to be living life more by design than by default.

His ability to find opportunity in everything inspired me to follow the entrepreneurial path as well.

Smitten with the idea of making money, I remember spending many hours scouring through *Small Business Opportunities* magazine. The majority of the magazine's readership probably wasn't 12 years old like I was, yet I drew lots of inspiration from it. I purchased a button-making machine (I learned about in the magazine) with the money I had earned as my dad's helper at his stand at the flea market. Then, I bought the latest teen magazines and cut out pictures of popular artists, making them into buttons that I sold for $1 each. Soon I had my own side hustle, and Dad gave me my own space to sell at his flea market table! As business grew, I began purchasing posters and other artist memorabilia to sell from my side of the table. I absolutely loved what I termed the "process of profit." I loved seeing the 50 cents I invested turn into a $1 or $1.50. I learned all about buying at wholesale and selling at retail. Soon, I added a line of sterling silver jewelry to my table—sourced from a jewelry wholesaler my savvy dad connected me with—and I was making a killing as my jewelry line had between a 300 and 500 percent markup.

Later, I began selling *Grit* magazine door-to-door, earning a commission on every sale. Although I was a shy introvert, I was motivated to make money and was able to put myself out there for the sake of yet another sale.

In the seventh grade, I began selling candy at school. Every morning Mom would give my sister and me $5 each to buy our lunch. On the way to school, I would take my $5 and purchase packs of candy. My favorite was Now and Later, but I also purchased Starburst and a variety of other candies. I would purchase the big packs for 50 cents, break them open, and sell each individually wrapped candy for 10 cents. By lunchtime, my $5 had grown to $15.

I did whatever I could think of for money. I even tried a landscaping business, cutting grass for local neighbors, until I figured out that manual labor just wasn't my thing.

Then, one day something happened that virtually altered the course and trajectory of my life. I heard the song "It's Like That" by Run-D.M.C. while visiting a friend. The year was 1983, and I was absolutely mesmerized by the song. It was pure poetry. I purchased the vinyl single and by my fiftieth listen, I decided that I was born to be a rap star. I purchased two turntables and a mixer and began to learn how to scratch and rap. Soon, I was creating mix tapes for the kids at school and selling them for $10 each. I even had the kids bring a blank tape to record onto, so I had zero overhead and my earnings were pure profit. The entrepreneurial spirit was going strong within me.

MY JOURNEY FROM W-2 TO 1099

I knew in my heart of hearts that forging my own path and making my own fortunes would be the life for me. In fact, the last time I received a W-2 or a paycheck from someone other than myself was more than 30 years ago. Until the age of 23, my entrepreneurial endeavors were just a side hustle while I maintained a regular job to ensure that I had a steady paycheck.

Although I had no formal education, I was really good at graphic design and my skills landed me a job at a small law firm. It was an unbelievably good career opportunity. The work was super easy and the pay was great, it gave me the autonomy I loved, and it was fun—the perfect job, am I right? But the job just didn't fulfill me in the way I desired. The content I was curating just wasn't my jam, and though the money was good, the job itself didn't give me a reason to leap out of bed every morning. As Tony Gaskins aptly put it, "if you don't build your dream, someone will hire you to build theirs."

My boss was Bryant Berry, one of the most successful bankruptcy attorneys in Austin, Texas, in the 1990s. Not only was he great at practicing law, but he spent countless hours researching law journals in order to stay up to date with the latest cases and rulings in bankruptcy law. He was what I affectionately call a "legal geek." His acumen for the legal game became so legendary that he attracted lawyers from all over the nation to pick his brain and learn how he took on so many successful cases. Mr. Berry's notoriety spun off into a burgeoning side career, and that's where I came in. He came up with the idea to put all of his studies and findings into a monthly newsletter and hired me to professionally design, print, and mail it to his subscriber base. Yes, snail mail—this was before the internet was a thing. Mr. Berry was also a master marketer and a wiz at lead generation, which kept his practice hopping and his acumen current and relevant.

Mr. Berry's subscribers would pay hundreds of dollars a year for his monthly newsletter so that they could save time foregoing the many hours of due diligence that he seemed to partake in for pleasure. Subscribing to Mr. Berry's newsletter allowed these attorneys to invest much more of their time and energy into making more money and helping more clients; it gave them a competitive advantage.

Going to work every day for someone else and helping him build his empire was a daily reminder of my own entrepreneurial aspirations. Eventually, the internal conflict that I felt became so great that I took action and gave my notice. When I finally cut the cord and became a full-time entrepreneur, it was to focus on a business idea I had started in my youth after hearing that fateful Run-D.M.C. song: record producing. But something became clear very quickly. I had no capital.

STRIKING OUT ON MY OWN

I needed $1,800 to record the first album under my new label, Grapetree Records, and I had an ingenious way to raise the money from family and friends. I wrote a template letter, in which I explained that I desired to launch my own business and that I wanted them to be a part of this new journey. Then, I broke the full amount of what I needed into what I called shares of $25 each. I included a coupon to fill out how many shares they wanted to purchase and included a self-addressed stamped envelope. The strategy worked! Some purchased 1 share while others donated 5 or 10. The funds I needed to launch came in very quickly.

As I recorded my album, I simultaneously launched a Christian rap magazine. In the beginning it was a one-man operation, and I handled everything from scheduling interviews with the artists to typing up the content, writing, layout, editing, and everything in between. Eventually, as the magazine became more successful—it was distributed in over 700 Christian bookstores—I began bringing on hired help. But I didn't quite know how to properly allocate my newly acquired help. I was in over my head. I was doing many of the right things, but I later learned that I was doing most of them in the wrong order.

Within a year, I had launched my own independent record label and began signing on artists. My little hobby had grown into a multipronged business, and I was working all the time. In fact, I would usually hit the office around 8 a.m. and I wouldn't be done with work until at least 10 p.m. I started neglecting everything important in my life for the sake of the business. All this business growth occurred during our first few years of marriage. My wife, Josie, would have dinner ready, and some-times she would have to heat up my food five times before I came in to eat because I would keep telling her, "I just need 15 more minutes!" My business quickly became my first love, and those things crept into our relationship and drove a little wedge between us. I was making a sacrifice, spending more time with the business than with my wife, with the premise that one day we would be so financially successful that we would have all the time in the world. After all, I was only 23 years old and I had my whole life ahead of me. What I didn't realize at the time was that I didn't own a business, *my business owned me!*

Looking back, I realize that because I experienced mental, physical, and emotional abuse growing up, a lot of my success was, in fact, a response to trauma. I was always trying to prove everyone wrong. I had been told from a very young age that I wasn't wanted and that I would never amount to anything, so I felt that I had to set the record straight. Because of my own feelings of unworthiness, I felt that I had to work all the time in order to make my mark and prove my naysayers wrong.

And prove them wrong I did. Fast forward six years and our little fledgling company was earning over $150,000 per month. We had 14 employees and 18 artists signed on and had become the world's number one Christian rap label by 1997. By the age of 29, I made my first million dollars. I felt like I had arrived, but I was still working just as long and hard as I had when I first started the business.

FROM RICHES TO RAGS

At the height of my record label's success, my wife and I were living in a 6,000-square-foot home that we had purchased when I was 26 years old. The home sat on 10 acres of land, where we built out a 1,500-square-foot office building and a 1,200-square-foot recording studio. It was quite an empire, and I felt like a king.

Then, right around the time I turned 31 years old, something I wouldn't have predicted happened: with the advent of digital music, our sales began to plummet. Instead of making our usual $130,000 to $160,000 per month, our sales dwindled over the following six months to less than $30,000 per month. As the entire US music market shifted to digital downloads, music sales tanked. Our payroll alone was $42,000 per month, and we were in trouble. No matter what I tried, I couldn't make ends meet. Eventually, we got the inevitable call from our distributor, EMI. They, too, had experienced the sting of the market and had decided to make some cuts, one of which was our label.

I tried to recover as best I could, but in the end my wife and I lost everything. Our home was in foreclosure, our life savings was exhausted, and we had no choice but to start over from scratch.

As we drove away from the property for the last time, I recall welling up with an overwhelming sense of failure, loss, and sorrow. I couldn't help but consider all of the opportunities I had forgone for the sake of building my kingdom. During the 10 years I spent climbing the ladder, my wife and I had only taken one vacation and I had probably worked an average of 70 hours a week. I knew there had to be a better way.

In 2003, at the age of 33, I completely reinvented myself and jumped into the real estate business. Although our home was in foreclosure, we put it on the market and got a solid offer just weeks before it was scheduled to go back to the bank. That summer, we closed the sale on the property. I still remember seeing the $29,397 I paid to the real estate agent on the settlement statement. As I reflected on what he had to do to sell it, I thought, Hey, maybe I can do that. It seemed to me that most of the work was done by his one assistant, and the rest of the work was done by the agent who brought in the offer. I began looking into becoming a real estate agent and I discovered that if I focused on working with sellers, I could build a very lucrative and highly leveraged business, one where others did most of the work and I still made a handsome payday.

I took the four required real estate classes over the course of two weeks, passed the exam to obtain my real estate license, and jumped into the real estate game.

This time I began working smarter versus harder; I found the business to be quite lucrative and fulfilling. By 2008, I was ranked by the *Austin Business Journal* as the number one real estate agent in Austin, Texas, out of more than 9,800 local agents. I was the king of my market, and not a single agent in the city could match my sales numbers. That year, I sold more than 100 homes as a solo agent, and I sold more than 1,000 homes during my first 10 years in the business.

In the real estate game, I was much more careful to allocate my time wisely. Josie and I began taking regular vacations. I took nights and weekends off and didn't work most Fridays. I had learned from my mistakes in my first business, but, in retrospect, I was still making tons of mistakes. While I was a master at generating business, I still was not working at maximum efficiency and I had not yet learned how to master money. As the saying goes, "You don't know what you don't know." Over time I learned how to work as little as possible while still maximizing my potential income.

THE THREE-HOUR DAY

About seven years ago, I traded in those long, hard hours for a much more sensible, efficient, and predictable schedule. I discovered that I can get far more done, and earn a lot more income, while simultaneously working a lot less. 3 Hours a Day was a huge breakthrough for me and has been an invaluable gift to my coaching clients. Today, I have more disposable income than I ever have, and I own multiple six-figure businesses that run with or without me.

Since adopting this lifestyle, I've been more at peace, spent more time with my family, enjoyed some of the richest experiences in life, and traveled the world, all while increasing my income.

Most of the entrepreneurs I coach are fairly successful. Many of them began entrepreneurship at a young age and have done well in many respects. Yet they still struggle with being continually bogged down by the minutia of their business. 3 Hours a Day is a supreme gift because it allows you to (1) discover who you are and what makes you happy, (2) pick two Big Picture Priorities that are in your zone of genius, and (3) delegate everything else to someone else.

I was told—and modeled—from a very early age that I had to work long and hard in order to make a decent living and enjoy a good life. I believed that the more you worked the more you earned. I have since learned the fallacy of that model.

WORK IN YOUR BUSINESS AND NOT ON IT

"You should be working in your business and not on it!"

I certainly can't remember the first time someone told me this, but I know I've heard it over and over again in my business journey. Chances are, if you've been in business for a while, you have, too. Yet, the truth is, no one has ever stopped to show me *how* to do this.

3 Hours a Day has become the ultimate solution to help me solve this conundrum, because it allows me to operate my life and business *above the maze*.

I thank God that along the way I discovered something quite interesting. Because I have always been a student of systems and efficiency, I began tracking what worked in my real estate business early on. From my incessant analysis, I could clearly see that about 10 to 15 percent of the things I was doing each day were really moving the needle in my business, while everything else was just putting out fires and maintaining the status quo. I discovered that I could hire folks to put out the fires and maintain the status quo, allowing me the freedom to work on the Big Picture Priorities that really propelled me to success. This strategy helped me to make my first million dollars at the age of 29 and has made me many millions since then. But more than that, it has helped me live life on my terms.

It is truly rare to find someone who lives the lifestyle that I live. There are entrepreneurs who make 10 times what I make, yet they are sorely lacking. They are rich on the outside, yet poor on the inside. They are missing out on the things that matter most in life. Then, there are those who make a smidgen of what I make, and yet they are stuck in the hustle and grind. It hasn't even crossed their mind that there could be a better way to live: A world where you make as much money as you desire, love what you do, work where you choose, and spend 90 percent of your week outside of your workday. This is the life I live every day, and it truly is the best life.

It is a scientific fact that you can become neurologically addicted to the hustle because it's an adrenaline rush.* But there are other ways to get that dopamine fix. I get a rush out of buying one-way tickets to my favorite world destinations and not

---

* Bryan Robinson, PhD, "The Addiction Nobody Talks About but Everybody Is Doing and 10 Solutions," *Forbes*, June 20, 2020, https://www.forbes.com/sites /bryanrobinson/2020/06/20/the-addiction-nobody-talks-about-but-everybody -is-doing-and-10-solutions/?sh=58f297f1467c.

knowing when I'll return home. My entire life is a rush. I know that as an entrepreneur, you are a rebel. You are always going to have a need to scratch that itch, but you don't have to scratch it by working 24/7 and killing yourself. It's just not worth it.

If you're an entrepreneur, would-be entrepreneur, or business leader that has been wounded or stuck in the weeds unable to grow, or you just feel like there is more to life than just work or business, this book is for you. You don't conform to the status quo and you don't have to. You can achieve your ultimate greatness and break through the glass ceiling without killing yourself. You might be afraid of what that looks like, but you can overcome your fears and lead a better, happier, more balanced life. You've put countless hours and tons of blood, sweat, and tears into your business, and it's gotten you this far. But sheer work ethic alone won't get you where you want to be. It's time to work smarter, not harder. It's time to transcend the hustle and grind.

I've told you my story to show that, no matter your background, experiencing the joy of 3 Hours a Day is possible, whether you work for someone else or work for yourself. So, whether you are a full-time entrepreneur, if you have a side hustle, or have been thinking about launching your own business, let's bring it on!

CHAPTER 2

Embracing 3 Hours a Day

I recently had a business-healing session with my client, Jackie, a real estate agent. I asked Jackie how much income she had earned during her best year in business. She grossed about $137,000. "How much time were you working?" I asked. Her response? "All the time." Had her business been following 3 Hours a Day, she could have earned far more than she did while working just a fraction of the time. In fact, in my own real estate practice, I was grossing quarterly more income than Jackie made in a year and I was only working a few hours a week.

The core concept of 3 Hours a Day is *focus*. It's about where you will spend your time and attention. Instead of starting off with the premise that you have eight work hours that day, and then filling those hours up with a bunch of activities that don't really move the needle for your business, limit yourself to three hours where you focus on just a few Big Picture Priorities that will move the needle the most.

In fact, you're missing a lot of business opportunities by not living this way. 3 Hours a Day will have you start thinking in a scaled way and force you to adopt *leverage*, meaning having the right people, systems, and tools (PST) in place, whether you have 1 or 1,000 people under you to delegate to. Having this in place will help you develop a vivid mental image of exactly where you intend your company to be in the next three to five years. Letting go and delegating is quite difficult at first, but once you learn and adopt my simple system, you'll be addicted to it, and it will revolutionize your business and your life. Not only that, but your family will love you for it.

To be clear, you are not going to make the leap to working 3 Hours a Day overnight, nor will you be expected to. Think about it like building a house. It can easily take nine months to a year to get your new custom home built and ready for occupancy. That nine months to a year is the hustle and grind. But after your home is built, you should be allowed to live in it and enjoy it. You should now be in a state of ease and flow. Sure, repairs will come up from time to time, and you will deal with those as they come. But, you can also delegate home repairs and routine maintenance. In the same way, while building your business will likely require some elbow grease in the beginning, you should be able to relax into a well-oiled machine within nine months to a year.

THE FUNDAMENTALS OF 3 HOURS A DAY

To get started on building that well-oiled machine, you will simply insert a three-hour slot within your current workday, replacing some of your non-income-producing activities with your new, shortened list of income-generating ones. Depending on where you are in your business, these activities may vary, but there will typically only be two main things that you are focused on: generating leads and scheduling appointments or making sales. (We will delve deeper into this in Step 6.) Eventually, you will begin delegating the most non-income-producing activities to others. In this way, 3 Hours a Day fits neatly into any work schedule.

Once you become more established, your two Big Picture Priorities will change from leads and appointments/sales to leading your team and building your brand (a.k.a., big picture lead generation). As you adopt 3 Hours a Day, you can choose to work a full three-hour block, but I think a better way of working on these tasks is to split them into two 90-minute chunks. I'll explain more about scheduling your day in Step 6.

WHY THE STANDARD EIGHT HOURS A DAY?

When you begin to live your life by design, you begin to question everything, including the things you may have taken for granted, like the concept of working eight hours a day. How did we get to the eight-hour workday to begin with, and is it really the best model in our current day and age?

The first law in the United States that called for an eight-hour workday was passed in Illinois in 1867. Before that, it wasn't uncommon for Americans to work 10 or 12 hours a day. Yet it wasn't until Henry Ford instituted an eight-hour workday for some of his employees in 1914 that the Illinois law stimulated a national discussion. More than seventy years after the Illinois law passed, President Franklin Roosevelt signed the Fair Labor Standards Act in 1938, legally requiring all full-time workers in the United States be paid overtime if they worked more than 40 hours a week.

While the industrial revolution led us to the standardized eight-hour workday, with all the technology, tools, and knowledge that we have now, we have been given the power to change how and where we work. Through the use of amazing leverage, you now have the power of choice. The eight-hour workday was created for employees, not entrepreneurs.

THE MYTHS OF THE THREE-HOUR DAY

As an entrepreneur, I suspect you have a very high work ethic and oftentimes you probably don't know what to do with yourself when you aren't working. From early childhood, we are conditioned to believe that hard work is *the way* to success, and doing it any other way feels like cheating.

Since most entrepreneurs believe that the hustle and grind is the only way to succeed, it is hard for some to accept that they can actually work far less and still enjoy a lavish lifestyle and phenomenal income. Even some of the most financially successful entrepreneurs go on to work long and hard well after they have earned the right to take it easy. Many have a stigma about being viewed as lazy, and some just don't know when to quit. The hustle and grind is certainly beneficial for a season, but it does not have to be an ongoing lifestyle choice. Some entrepreneurs never received that memo.

And I understand, it's difficult to rewire your brain to the opposite of what society has conditioned you to believe. When you study the life of social insects like ants and bees, you will see that they appear to be working all the time. As social beings, humans also derive much fulfillment out of working, accomplishing tasks, and being involved in various projects. 3 Hours a Day allows you to live a more balanced life. It doesn't take away your sense of purpose, but enhances it. Living your life by design is truly the epitome of living your life on purpose.

With this in mind, let's break down the six major, self-limiting beliefs surrounding 3 Hours a Day.

Myth 1: "There's NO WAY!"

The first myth that I often hear from entrepreneurs who have been overworking is, "There's no way you could possibly work three hours a day and still make six or seven figures." The truth is many thousands of entrepreneurs are already doing it.

Sadly, many entrepreneurs have been disillusioned, forgetting why they got into business in the first place. If you're like most, you got into business because you wanted to do something that you loved and you wanted to do it on your own terms. You wanted to work on your own schedule without limiting your income.

By having the right PST, as discussed earlier in the chapter and as we will discuss further in Steps 4 and 5, you can free up your time so that you can return to your original mission and vision. You will also be free to alter the course of your life. You can now move on from being an unbridled workaholic to a person of balance, ease, and flow.

Myth 2: "I Could NEVER Work That Schedule"

Some entrepreneurs have the preconceived notion that with 3 Hours a Day you HAVE to stop everything immediately and quit your regular schedule cold turkey. While that will likely be your ultimate goal, you will actually start by inserting 3 Hours a Day into your current schedule. You will carve out 3 Hours a Day for income-producing and wealth-generating activities. Through proper delegation, eventually you will get to a point where you need to work less and less.

Countless entrepreneurs practicing this movement are embracing and loving this schedule, and they are living balanced and fulfilled lives as a result. It's hard at first for many of my students to understand that working all the time with no end in sight is damaging to their goals. It's time to incorporate discipline. Most entrepreneurs despise authority and rules, so discipline may not sit very well with you at first. But what I'm talking about is not some outside authority telling you what to do. Instead, it's YOU creating a code of conduct that will lead to your ultimate success.

In a 3 Hours a Day lifestyle, discipline simply involves you creating and maintaining a schedule. Will you work from 9 a.m. to noon or will you work two 90-minute shifts, spread throughout the day? Will you begin by incorporating your 3 Hours a Day into your eight-hour schedule, or will you trim your schedule down to six hours? The choice is yours.

It is ironic that entrepreneurs will question the idea of working 3 Hours a Day, yet they take at face value a schedule that was standardized by Henry Ford more than 100 years ago. How modern is that? Every major field has advanced more in the past 100 years than in all of recorded history combined. Yet the workday has gone on for more than 100 years without an upgrade. It is no longer necessary to work 8 to 12 hours a day to achieve your goals. You are now free to work just three hours a day and accomplish everything your heart desires.

Myth 3: "Leverage COSTS TOO MUCH"

This myth is a big one for many of my coaching clients when they first come to me. Perhaps you've told yourself that you don't have help because you believe you can't afford it. But the truth is, you can't afford not to have leverage. Countless studies have shown the negative effects of working more than you should. Doing it all is killing you . . . literally.

Your first hire will typically be the opposite of you. What I mean by that is that their personality profile will most likely be the opposite of yours. They will be responsible for all of the minutia in your business. These are the things that obviously must get done but don't need to be done by you. I'm telling you right here and now that 90 percent of the activities that are happening in your business *do not* need to be done by you. Instead, they should be delegated.

OK, don't freak out! Catch your breath and let that sink in. The way that you will get your time back is by delegating 90 percent of the activities that you currently do. I know it's scary, but it's also necessary. It's high time that you scrape your plate.

OK, Knolly I get it. But how am I going to pay someone when I don't have the money for their salary? Ah! Great question! Are you ready to get creative?

The solution is actually quite simple when you reframe it: instead of stating that you can't afford to pay someone, ask yourself, How can I afford to pay someone? Now you are entering into a realm of creativity and power. Choice is now back in your court and the possibilities are limitless.

The truth is you don't have to have the money to pay someone. You simply have to *create* the money to pay someone. Better yet, *they* have to create the money to pay themselves.

Does it sound like I'm speaking a foreign language?

Let me share my simple solution to your dilemma. This is the kind of gold that my coaching clients pay thousands of dollars for! I will get into specifics on hiring in Step 4, so I'll just share a few basic premises here.

All of my staff members are virtual assistants (VAs). I currently have four on my payroll. Three of them live in the Philippines and one lives in the United States. Hiring a VA from outside the US means that I am now getting a highly qualified person at a cost of about $5 to $6 an hour (sometimes less). When I hire someone to work for 30 hours per week, my cost will be $792 per month on the high end (that's six hours a day × $6 per hour × 22 workdays in a month).

I already know what you're thinking. You get what you pay for. Yes and no. Since the rate of exchange to the US dollar is quite favorable in the Philippines, my VAs are making really good money. They also get to work from home, and they have a great boss to boot! If you pick the right agency to source your VA, you will typically have four or five candidates to interview and all will be the cream of the crop.

One of my VAs has been with me for eight years, another has been with me for seven years, and the other two have been with me for four years, so they are all long-term hires. Plus, they all have college degrees and are amazing at what they do. And believe me when I say that my VAs run my organization.

So, let's say you budget $800 per month for your admin person. Now, all you have to do is create a small project or sales funnel, which your admin will be in charge of, that will generate $1,000 a month in additional income. You can have that individual run this new project utilizing just 10 percent of their workday. Now, your VA is completely paid for through a project that they oversee during just a fraction of their day, leaving 90 percent of their time available to dedicate to the activities you hired them for.

It's not free labor; it's leveraged labor. Let me give you three ideas to help spark your creative juices:

Idea 1: You could agree to coach a fellow entrepreneur who is struggling in an area you've already mastered. If you charged $1,000 per month for 30 minutes (or one hour per week) of one-on-one coaching, your VA is paid for, and it only requires a few hours a month of your time.

Idea 2: You could create a group coaching program and charge $97 per month per student. Once you have 10 students in your program, your VA is paid for and you are only investing one hour a week on your weekly Zoom call! Best of all, your VA will be in charge of sending out the emails, texts, and phone calls to get the students into the program, as well as handling all the back-end administration.

Idea 3: You could create a digital bootcamp that you sell for $297. Run some Facebook ads or market directly to your industry. If you sell just three units per month, your VA is paid for. Of course, your VA will be in charge of running the ads and administrating the entire program, which should only take about 30 minutes a day. To see a living example of this, go to KnollyBootcamp.com.

Now it's time to come up with your own ideas for how to pay for your VA. Involve your business partner or your life partner in this process, or hire someone to coach you on this. When you understand the principle, there are literally 101 different ways you can create the revenue you need to pay for your admin person. This is literally how I have funded my team for the past seven years. You'll have your team run these additional revenue streams so they are truly paying for themselves. Now you no longer have an excuse to kill yourself doing the things that others should be doing for you.

Myth 4: "I'm Not ORGANIZED"

Because I am a master at systems and organization, many entrepreneurs and business leaders have hired me over the years to help them systematize and organize their business. Organizing your business is easier than you think, and in Step 5, I will take you through an easy-to-implement process that will finally have your business systematized and humming like a well-oiled machine.

I cannot take credit for my skills as an organizational wizard. Although meticulously nurtured, it's a gift that I was born with.

Having an organized and systematized business that runs with or without you is quintessential to your success in following 3 Hours a Day. Yet the shocking truth is YOU don't ever have to become organized. Sure, it will probably help for you to become a *little* more organized than you are, but you never have to become a master at organization. In fact, you can feel free to remain as unorganized as you like.

The DISC personality assessment, based on the emotional and behavioral theory of psychologist William Moulton Marston, breaks down personalities into four different sections: (D)ominance, (I)nfluence, (S)teadiness, and (C)onscientiousness. It takes a good amount of S and C to be naturally gifted at systems and organization. However, most entrepreneurs test particularly high in D or I on the personality scale. Typically, they are a combination of both. While anyone can learn to become more organized, I'm going to teach you to lean into your natural strengths, polishing them and becoming a master at your natural gifts.

Following your natural proclivities based on your personality profile will not only make your entrepreneurial journey easier, it will also make everything you do more fun. That's because you are only doing the things that you really like or love. Is your natural proclivity to be disorganized? No problem! You can hire somebody at $6 an hour who is naturally gifted at organization and systems, and help them lean into their gifts to the benefit of your enterprise. Being disorganized will never again be an excuse for you to continue to stifle the growth of your success.

If you are not aware of what your personality profile is, I have included a number of free profile tests that you can find in the

Resources section at the back of the book. For more information about the DISC assessment, and to take the assessment yourself, visit 3HoursADay.com/bookresources.

Myth 5: "I've Had BAD EXPERIENCES Hiring People"

So, you've hired someone in the past and they absolutely sucked. You were overwhelmed at the time and needed to scrape your plate, and you hired someone out of desperation but found that you had to keep taking their job back. After all, when you want something done right, shouldn't you just do it yourself?

Yes, I get it. You are the only one in the world capable of doing your job. There is no one on the planet as good as you. I'm already picturing a slow-motion video of you hard at work with the chorus to Carly Simon's "Nobody Does it Better" blaring in the background. If you cannot move past the myth that you have to do everything yourself, then your company will be doomed to stay smaller than it wants to be, and you won't be able to realize the ultimate freedom of your time, finances, and location.

The folks you are hiring are not stifling the success of your business; you are. That's because you are acting as the bottleneck to your own growth.

Let's say you've been doing what you do for the past 10 years. You've already clocked thousands of hours on the road to mastery and you are damn good. But you know you need help, so you bring on someone and train them for a few hours (or maybe a week) and then set them loose. You put in your 10,000 hours, but you've trained them for just 10 hours . . . and you wonder why they suck.

I recently sat down for a 1:1 session with Lisa, one of my coaching clients. She happens to be in real estate sales, and in that space my success is well known. Lisa was having trouble getting consistent quality work out of her VA so that she could truly scrape her plate and begin enjoying the benefits of 3 Hours a Day.

"Let me ask you a question, Lisa," I said. "If you were to bring me into your organization to oversee it for a few months, do you believe that I could get it running proficiently for you, drastically increasing both your revenue and your profits?"

Lisa perked up. "Of course, Knolly! If I had you running my operation I know it would be much more successful."

"Well then," I explained, "you don't really have an issue with your VA. You have a leadership/training issue. It isn't that your VA sucks, it's that YOU suck."

While this truth may sound harsh, sadly, it's true. In Step 4, I will explain the reason why most entrepreneurs don't do well with hiring, and throughout this book I will show you how to fix this problem once and for all.

Myth 6: "I Like to WORK!"

As a recovering workaholic myself, this myth is a really tough one to tackle. As entrepreneurs, it almost feels like we are *wired to work*. While this may seem true, it's actually false in the grand scheme.

Perhaps you absolutely love what you do, so much that you consider it play and do not have a clearly visible line of demarcation between the two. When you go on vacation, you would rather be working because, for you, work is more fun. Well, either you are slightly masochistic or you are one of the rare lucky ones who has landed on your purpose and passion. Good for you! You find the deepest meaning in what you do. Only a small percentage of the population is walking in their purpose, and you've found yours.

Even so, I would argue that it is not so much your work itself that you love, rather it is the *feeling* you are deriving from the work. While it is true that you are fulfilling your passion and purpose, it is also true that there is a deep sense of fulfillment that you are contriving from doing this work.

This was the case for me. I could work anywhere from 12 to 14 hours a day for weeks on end, and for the most part, I loved every minute of it. For me, delegating tasks that I didn't like simply freed me up to work even more on the things I loved. It felt almost as though I was wired for work.

The major problem you are setting yourself up for when you overwork is burnout. Make no mistake, there will eventually be a blowback. Even if you are doing the Lord's work, there comes a point at which enough is enough. What I have found necessary for my coaching clients in this situation is a process that I call "rechanneling." Rechanneling, as I teach it, is the process of discovering how you are wired and taping into your passion and purpose. You can then channel your passion and purpose through all areas of your life, so that it's not just your work that brings you fulfillment. This is a more balanced approach.

For the past 30 years, the majority of my teaching and training has been centered around helping entrepreneurs and leaders find their purpose. When someone truly discovers their divine destiny it is a monumental achievement! I have found, though, that many will push this to the extremes, working all the time since it is for a *good cause*. I don't believe that we are here primarily to work. We are here to experience life first and foremost. Again, we are human *beings*, not human doings.

If you like to work all the time and you are getting some form of emotional satisfaction out of working, your workaholism could also be a direct result of a trauma response. I know, because I've been through it, and it motivated me to work harder to escape that trauma.

My mother suffers with emotional illness, and being raised by her wasn't easy. My sister and I spent much of our childhood with Mom, and we suffered through severe physical, mental, and emotional abuse. Mom was angry with Dad. Since I reminded her of him, I felt that, at times, she hated me. Not only did I look like Dad, but I bore his name! I am Knolly Alexander Williams, Jr., yet my mom never, ever has called me by my first name. Sometimes, I would get slapped across the room just because I looked like Dad. She would remind me repeatedly that I was a mistake and that she should never have had me. She also made sure I knew that I was worthless and would never amount to anything. Consequently, I spent much of my life subconsciously trying to prove Mom wrong. Through the accumulation of wealth, I was trying to prove to my mom that I *was* worth having and that I could be a success. In truth, I was simply trying to prove this to myself, because my subconscious mind had purchased the lies I was sold as a youth.

Eventually, I came to realize that I absolutely am worthy of everything this life has for me, for no other reason than the fact I was born into this realm. I no longer have to prove my worth to myself or anyone else. Find out exactly what emotions are being fulfilled through *your* work and then discover other ways to fulfill or eliminate those emotional needs. Once you reframe and rewrite your story, you can begin to channel your passion for work into some of the other 14 life areas which have probably been neglected. I'll cover this more in Step 2.

TIME TO SUIT UP!

What all these myths have in common is that they seem to make perfect sense, but only to the unexpanded brain. Common, everyday folk love to make excuses for why they live mundane, mediocre, and unextraordinary lives. But you are anything but average. You are an extraordinary entrepreneur.

I encourage you to move past the common myths that will hold you back from experiencing the most amazing journey possible on this planet. The journey begins with you taking ownership of who you really are. It's time to suit up and hone your superpower!

CHAPTER 3

Step 1:
Hone Your Superpower

We now come to Step 1 in the seven-step process to your 3 Hours a Day: discovering and honing your superpower. This is a foundational step that many entrepreneurs unwisely skip, and subsequently go on to build an entire empire on very shaky ground. They dedicate countless hours to building companies, empires, and legacies while completely missing the ultimate mark. When you tap into your superpower and build your business and life around it, ease and flow is the natural result.

Growing up, I used to watch *Justice League*. Batman, Superman, Wonder Woman, and others would band together as a team to fight evil. Each superhero brought a unique superpower to the table, and each of them was really good in a specific skill. And while they are powerful when working on their own, they become legendary when they team up and pool their skills together. In the same way Batman and Superman can combine their brains and brawn to successfully fight crime, you can use your own particular strengths—and find those who complement them—to succeed.

Knowing your superpower also shines a huge spotlight on your weaknesses. This will seem uncomfortable at first, but believe me when I say it is actually incredibly freeing. As you hone your superpower and lean into it, you will also begin to see which areas you're not as strong in and can use that to figure out what qualities to look for in a partner to help complement those areas and become unstoppable. But before you can become unstoppable, you have to set some goals for yourself and your business.

WHAT DO YOU WANT?

Finding your life's passion and purpose is a topic that I love teaching. I really like knowing what makes people tick, so "What do you want?" is a question that I often ask folks in casual conversation. Most people just look at me as if it were a trick question. It's not. The question is simple enough, but the answer can be elusive. That's because most people have never taken the time to really get to know themselves and understand exactly what creates deep, lasting, and optimal happiness for them.

In most goal-setting exercises, the majority of my students begin answering the question by throwing out a monetary figure. Some will answer, "I want to earn $100,000 a year." Others might say, "I want to generate 40 clients a year." While both of these answers are worthy and attainable objectives, true goal setting begins at a much deeper level.

Years ago, I was casually loafing around in my living room with a close friend. He began telling me in great detail how much he hated his job, how unfair his supervisors were, and how little he was paid for the enormous amount of responsibility he shouldered. Rather than weigh in on his pity party fueled by a victim mindset, I simply popped the question, "What do you want?" Silence. My friend looked back at me with a blank stare, completely taken aback. As I listened to him passionately speak about everything he did not want, I simply had to know, "What do you want?" Although he could speak for several minutes straight about all the things that he did not want in life, this simple question seemed to completely stump him.

As with any noble mission or grand objective, 3 Hours a Day begins with setting your goals. In order to set accurate goals, you have to know exactly what you want.

The Four Groups of People

What does success look like? Is a man with a $500 million net worth a success? What about a woman who lived day-to-day with no money in her bank account? Would you think she was a success? I have come to understand that, generally speaking, there are four different groups of people:

- **GROUP 1.** Those who don't know what they want.
- **GROUP 2.** Those who know what they want but are afraid to pursue it.
- **GROUP 3.** Those who think they know what they want but really don't.
- **GROUP 4.** Those who really know what they want and pursue it.

Let's break them down:

GROUP 1. Those Who Don't Know What They Want.
This group includes the vast army of entrepreneurs who have never taken the time to become self-aware. These

people often busy themselves with trying to please others or trying to be like others. They don't really know where they fit in, so they just go with the flow. They fall into the cracks.

GROUP 2. Those Who Know What They Want but Are Afraid to Pursue It.
In my opinion, this group is worse off than the first. They actually have (or once had) a dream and a purpose, but they are afraid to go after it. It is shameful to squander the one life we are given in pursuit of anything other than our true purpose.

GROUP 3. Those Who Think They Know What They Want but Really Don't.
This group starts out delusional and ends up disillusioned. Yet, because they do have goals and aspirations, they can oftentimes look extremely successful on the outside. They pursue a career that is not a good fit for them in exchange for fortune, fame, to please another, or for some equally worthless reason. In their life, they have all the stuff and lots of fluff, but no substance. They are a big beautiful ship navigating the wrong seas and charting the wrong course.

GROUP 4. Those Who Really Know What They Want and Pursue It.
These are the happy ones. On the outside, they can look like a wild success, a miserable failure, or anything in between. Nevertheless, on the inside they are full and fulfilled. This group represents those who are truly successful.

It's important to understand that, for those in Group 4, success looks different for each person, because what we want is unique. You should forsake the path you are on if it is not leading you where you want to be. You can be a billionaire and be successful. At the same time, you can live like Mother Teresa, who took a vow of poverty, and be a success.

DISCOVERING YOUR DESTINY

All of my training and experience has led me to believe that human beings are on this planet for three primary reasons: (1) to have an experience (to be), (2) to fulfill a mission (to do), and (3) to leave a legacy (to give). What is your passion? What is your purpose? What do you want?

To get to the heart of what you really want, consider these questions:

- If you could do or be anything in the world, what would you do or be?
- What would you do for free (i.e., without pay)?
- If you had $10 million in the bank and didn't have to work, what would you do?

Experiencing ultimate greatness begins with knowing who you are and why you are here. I call this "destiny discovery."

I have been obsessed with sharing this knowledge for the past 30 years. I even filmed an eight-week online training series called *Discovering Your Divine Destiny* while Josie and I were out traveling Europe. This course has refreshed and revolutionized the lives of many entrepreneurs. While a comprehensive destiny discovery course is outside of the scope of this book, it is an important first step to 3 Hours a Day, because understanding who you are and why you are here is essential to understanding your superpower. When you tap into your superpower and build your business and life *around* it, ease and flow is the natural result. Let me share the components of my *Discovering Your Divine Destiny Workbook* with you.

DISCOVERING YOUR SUPERPOWER

In this streamlined version of my *Discovering Your Divine Destiny Workbook*, you will discover your superpower through a series of questions mapped out into five categories. If you already know what your superpower is, play along anyway! You will gain some powerful insights to help you lean more fully into it and maximize your effectiveness.

If you find that going through this exercise is difficult and exhausting, you are not alone. Since I have been practicing destiny discovery and working on becoming the ultimate version of myself for many years, this work comes natural to me, but if you have never taken the time to dig in and do this work, it can be very painful.

It is quite natural and common to not want to take such a careful look at yourself, so if you find the following questions too difficult to navigate on your own, I highly recommend that you hire a coach who can assist you in doing this, so that you can enjoy maximum fulfillment on your journey to 3 Hours a Day.

EXERCISES

1. DISCOVERING YOUR DIVINE DESIGN

Answer all of the questions in each category to create an inventory of your life purpose. These questions will reveal what you already know about your superpower and provide you with a great baseline for your journey toward discovering your life purpose.

Inner Knowing

This is your internal sense of who you feel you really are:

- In your heart of hearts, what do you already know about who you were created to be?
- During your life up to this point, what types of activities have brought you the deepest sense of meaning and purpose?
- If you had $10 million in the bank and the freedom to become whatever you wanted to, what would you become?
- According to what you already know about your skill set, what does it appear that you were designed for?

Roles and Responsibilites

Let's take a look at and assess your past roles and responsibilities.

List 5 to 10 roles and/or responsibilities that you really enjoy and feel you are good at:

1. _____

2. _____

3. _____

4. _____

5. _____

6. _____

7. _____

8. _____

9. _____

10. _____

Now, circle your top three favorite roles from the list above.

List 5 to 10 roles and/or responsibilities that you know you are NOT good at:

1. _____

2. _____

3. _____

4. _____

5. _____

6. _____

7. _____

8. _____

9. _____

10. _____

Now, circle your three least favorite roles from the list above.

Affirmation/Feedback

When we are moving within our divine purpose, we will often receive positive affirmations and feedback from the people around us:

- What do those who know you the best say about what you were made to do?
- Name some times when you have been greatly affirmed in who you are and what you were born for.
- What have you done that has been the most beneficial to others?
- What relationships or people have influenced your sense of destiny? In what ways?

Personality Assessment

You were designed with a unique personality profile. Understanding your personality will go a long way toward helping you understand your divine destiny:

- Do you know your personality type from DISC, Genius Test, or some other system?
- If so, what have you learned from your personality assessment about who you are? Important: If you have not yet taken your personality profile assessment, take some time to complete your free online DISC profile. You can get an updated link to a free online DISC test at 3HoursADay .com/bookresources. Study the results carefully BEFORE moving on.

Strengths and Weaknesses

Your strengths are connected with your destiny. Name several things that you are really good at (your best talents and natural abilities).

List 5 to 10 of your key strengths:

1. _____
2. _____
3. _____
4. _____
5. _____
6. _____
7. _____
8. _____
9. _____
10. _____

List 5 to 10 of your biggest weaknesses:

1. _____
2. _____
3. _____
4. _____
5. _____
6. _____

7. _____

8. _____

9. _____

10. _____

2. DISCOVERING YOUR DIVINE PASSION

Everyone has things that motivate, inspire, energize, and light their passion. Let's discover YOURS!

My Passion

- What are you most passionate about?
- What gives you a reason to get up in the morning?
- If you could live your life doing one thing, what would it be?
- What fills your whole being with energy?
- What causes do you see around you that you want to fight for or against?

List three things you've done that you couldn't wait to get to each day:

1. _____

2. _____

3. _____

List three things you've dreaded and constantly wanted to avoid:

1. _____

2. _____

3. _____

My Fulfillment

Thinking about things you have done in the past, what has been the most satisfying thing you have done?

- What made it so fulfilling?
- What have you done in life that you'd love to do more of?
- What have you done that you are most proud of?
- What makes you feel fully alive when you are doing it?
- What have you done that gives you the feeling of being right in the *sweet spot* of life?

Changing the World

- What issues do you truly care about in the world around you?
- If you could invest the rest of your life and know you could change one thing in the world around you, what would it be?
- Imagine yourself at the end of your life looking back. What do you dream of doing to serve or help others that would cause you deep regret if you never took the risk to go for it?

3. DISCOVERING YOUR DIVINE DESIRES

Your dreams and desires are highly personal. Therefore, no matter how fantastic or unbelievable they may seem, you should take the time during this section to articulate them in as much detail as possible!

- What would you like to do in this life? Remember that your dreams can be large or small, significant or just for fun—for others or for you. What do you dream of doing?
- Write down some of your bigger dreams. These are dreams that seem farther off or might take a while to realize.
- If you had unlimited resources and couldn't fail, what would you set out to do?

- Is there a dream that you are afraid to voice, maybe for fear that you might look arrogant or presumptuous, or you won't be able to do it?
- Now take a look at the dreams you've written down. What would your dreams look like if you used your full capacity? If you dreamed in terms of your potential instead of your current capabilities, how would your dream change?

Dreaming for Fun

- What do you want to build or create in your lifetime, just for the joy of creativity?
- Where would you like to go in your life? What would you like to see and do?
- What do you want to learn? What skills do you want to master?

List some things you'd like to do in life purely for the fun of it:

- _____
- _____
- _____
- _____
- _____
- _____
- _____
- _____
- _____
- _____

Regrets

- Imagine you are 80 years old and looking back at your life. What dream from your list would cause the greatest regret if you had NOT pursued it?
- Let's say you stay on your current career/life path until the day you retire. If you were looking back on that life, how would you feel about it?
- What will you lose if you stay safe, stay here, and don't chase your dreams?

Use the questions above to create a list of dreams to pursue before you die. Don't place any judgment on the answers that spring to mind. Be completely open and free to jot down whatever is in your heart (whatever comes to mind). These are dreams that could happen, not goals that must be pursued.

4. DISCOVERING YOUR DIVINE EXPERIENCES

During this part of the exercise, we are going to examine your life experiences to see how they have prepared you for your divine destiny.

When considering your life experiences, I would like you to be open to the idea that all of your experiences (whether they be perceived as good or bad, successes or failures) have played a role in preparing you for the divine destiny and purpose for which you were fashioned.

Past Experience

- What has your whole life prepared you to do?
- Don't just think work—combine all your experiences, from all areas of life. What kind of role or task would bring all the best of what you've learned in life to the forefront?

- What experiences have most shaped who you are as a person? How have those changes prepared you for what you most want to do in life?

Failures

- At their point of need, people are most open to being influenced by someone who's gone through what they have. Given that, WHO has your life prepared you to serve?
- What opportunities have your mistakes made available to you that wouldn't have come had you succeeded?
- What gifts have your failures given you?

Work Experience

- What knowledge or skills have you acquired in your career that you want to incorporate as you pursue your purpose in life?
- What have you accomplished in your career that you are most proud of?

List five work experiences that have readied you for your destiny:

1. _____

2. _____

3. _____

4. _____

5. _____

How have these experiences prepared you to do what you were born to do?

Skills and Abilities

- If you were hiring yourself, what job would your experience best qualify you for?
- What kinds of things are people always asking you to do for them? (In other words, which of your skills do others consistently recognize as valuable?)
- What can you do, or do in a unique way, that almost no one else can?
- List two or three examples of skills you've picked up that have made a big difference in the trajectory of your life.

What are the five most important skills you will need to fully live out your life purpose?

1. _____

2. _____

3. _____

4. _____

5. _____

On a scale of 1 to 10, what is your level of competency in each of the skills listed above?

List some of your key learned skills:

- _____
- _____
- _____
- _____
- _____
- _____
- _____
- _____
- _____

List five of your top skills and abilities, in terms of how useful they are to you:

1. _____
2. _____
3. _____
4. _____
5. _____

5. DISCOVERING YOUR DIVINE CALLING

Calling can be defined as a commission coming from outside of yourself, to serve something bigger than yourself.

What do you care most about that is bigger than you? It can be a cause, a goal, a principle, a people, a truth—what do you want to give your life to?

- What world-changing dream makes your heart beat faster?
- Thinking about your legacy, what form will it take? Will it be people you've invested in, building an organization, something you've created, your family heritage, or something else?
- If you could spend your life working to change one thing in the world that would make a real difference for others, what would that one thing be?
- Imagine you were at the end of your life looking back. What deeds would enable you to honestly say, "That was a life well lived!"?

Who Will You Serve?

- Who do you want to help in your life? Is there a person or client avatar, for whom you would like to make a difference?
- Think back over the last 90 days. Who have you gone out of your way to help, in big ways or small? What drew you to each of those people?
- What causes fire you up? It could be the environment, adoption, digging wells in Africa, animal rescue, human rights, making your neighborhood safe, anything. What cause gets you angry, passionate, determined, or excited?
- In what areas do you repeatedly find others looking to you for hope, wisdom, service, or a touch of love? How does it touch your heart when they come to you?

Service from Suffering

- What individuals, groups, or needs do you identify with out of your own suffering? How do you want to help them?
- Where in life have you been most deeply hurt? How could you turn that energy toward helping others in similar situations?
- What areas of your life that were previously broken or messed up are you now using to help others? What messages of hope does your life embody for others?

• • •

I pray that this introductory workbook has helped you understand more about who you are, how you are wired, and why you are here. I also recommend that you take a series of free personality tests, which I have included at 3HoursaDay.com /bookresources.

Please do not underestimate the importance of honing your superpower. Too many of my clients want to jump ahead to the "good stuff." This *is* the good stuff. Discovering who you are is a critical first step to fulfilling your purpose on this earth. Happiness is a byproduct of living your purpose. Therefore it is imperative that you understand what your purpose is and live it.

Now it's time for us to evaluate your business, so that we can see exactly where it is and begin your transformation to 3 Hours a Day.

CHAPTER 4

Step 2:
Evaluate Your Business

Now that you know exactly what your superpower is and are leaning fully into it, it's time to evaluate exactly where you *are* in your business so that we can begin to work on what matters most. You cannot fully enjoy the incredible benefits of 3 Hours a Day without first doing some soul searching (which we did in Chapter 3) and then cleaning house (which we will do in this chapter). This step involves a cold hard look at exactly where you are so that you can move on to the success that you desire.

DIAGNOSING THE PROBLEM

Among many things, my dad was a master mechanic. He worked on classic and antique cars, and he really was a genius at it. I often joked that Dad could take apart an entire '55 Oldsmobile engine, spread all the parts across the driveway, and put it all back together again before dinnertime without reading a single line of a Haynes or Chilton manual. He seemed to have a photographic memory when it came to taking things apart and putting them back together. But what he really needed the most help with was *diagnosing* the problem.

If one of his vehicles was malfunctioning, he would narrow the problem down to a few things that could possibly be wrong and then take it to an auto shop for testing and a second opinion. The mechanic at the auto shop would run a thorough diagnostic on the vehicle, determine exactly what the problem was, and let Dad know how much it would cost to fix. Of course, Dad would never let on that he was a mechanic himself. He simply didn't own the expensive diagnostic systems or have the expertise that was required to zero in on the exact issue. Once the shop performed his evaluation and gave Dad an estimate, he would let them know that he would "think on it," and from there he would head straight to the auto parts store. After purchasing everything he needed to do the job, he would head home and fix up the vehicle in a jiffy.

While many of my students are genius entrepreneurs, most have never quite gotten the knack of evaluating exactly what issues in their business need fixing and plugging the holes. In this step, you are going to do just that. Business and life cannot be separated, because they are one and the same. Entrepreneurship is simply another facet of your life story. You and I are going to take a brutal and honest look at your business, and while we're at it we are going to take a gander at your life.

THE FIVE AREAS

When is the last time you took a good hard look at the major areas of your business in order to understand where gaps might exist? It's common for entrepreneurs to spend a great deal of time mapping out their business ideas before they start a company. Likewise, I believe that the evaluation process should continue throughout the life of your business and be done on, *at least*, a quarterly basis. When is the last time you did a thorough evaluation of your business?

Over the years, I have utilized a variety of different strategies for evaluating my businesses, but I learned my favorite strategy from my client James Friel. James is an investor, entrepreneur, and consultant who helps entrepreneurs systemize, grow, and scale their businesses by getting them out of the day-to-day operations of running their companies so they can make more money and have more time and freedom.

I met James through our mutual friend Nicholas Bayerle, CEO of the King's Brotherhood and best-selling author of, *The Modern Day Business Man*. When I was a real estate broker in Austin, I helped both Nicholas and James relocate to the city. At one of the Brotherhood conferences, James came in as a speaker. He laid out a simplified plan for evaluating the five areas of your business: marketing, sales, delivery, operations, and finance. It's really quite clever. Let's break down the five areas:

Marketing: The essence of marketing is understanding your market and figuring out what your consumers want. In his book *Breakthrough Advertising*, Eugene Schwartz posited the idea that you are channeling the existing desire of a market into your product or service. Marketing is always about your prospect, not your product.

Sales: Sales is about *how* you are solving the problem of your prospect. What is the big itch they need to scratch? What is the problem they desperately need to solve? What are they most interested in? This is your mechanism to convert interest into sales. With sales, you are articulating your value proposition and you are converting value into cash.

Delivery: This is where you deliver your product or service. You are delivering on the promise you made during your marketing and sales activities. Depending on your product or service, your delivery method can be automated, digital, manual, or physical. It's about how you are getting your product or service to your customers and clients.

Operations: This is all of your back-end systems. This area can include your product and customer support, your employees and contractors, systems, tools, platforms, and procedures. This area is about the way you are operating your business.

Finance: Finance is how we keep track of how we are doing; it's essentially how we keep score. This area involves setting and tracking your production goals and your financial goals. It's where you measure your results against your expectations.

Now, I want you to take a good look at these five areas in your business specifically. Here, it's time for personal reflection. As you answer the key questions below, I want you to assign each area a color of RED, YELLOW, or GREEN.

RED = I have to do it all.
YELLOW = A few things are working but I have to keep jumping back in and putting out fires.
GREEN = Everything is dialed in and I can manage it by looking at a number.

Don't overthink this small exercise. Once you know where your business is in any particular area, simply write R, Y, or G next to it. This evaluation process further helps you decide which areas of your business need the most help so that you can choose what to work on first. When you approach it honestly, the evaluation process can be quite eye-opening.

Remember that this first step is about *evaluating*, not *judging*. At this juncture, you aren't going to judge your business or even try to fix it. You are simply observing what is. We will work to balance your business in the next chapter. For now, we are just taking a good look under the hood. Eventually, in order to fully enjoy 3 Hours a Day, you will want to be at a GREEN level in each area.

Marketing:
- How great is my marketing acumen?
- Do I thoroughly understand my market?
- Have I identified my ideal client?
- How well do I know what my clients want?

Sales:
- What specific problem(s) am I solving with my product/service?
- How do I articulate my value proposition?
- Why should a prospect hire me over any of my competitors?
- What skills do I need to acquire in order to be the best at sales?

Delivery:
- Do I consistently deliver on my promises to my clients?
- Do I meet or exceed my client's expectations most of the time?

- Is my current average delivery time agreeable to my clients and prospects?
- What can I do to improve on the delivery of my product/service?

Operations:

- Is my operation running smoothly?
- Are my current tools and systems modern and up to date?
- Do I have the best systems in place?
- In what ways can I improve my back-end operations?

Finance:

- Am I meeting or exceeding my financial goals?
- Do I have consistent cash flow?
- Have I built a pipeline/funnel of business such that revenue is steadily flowing into my company?
- Is my company steadily growing financially year over year?

THE LIFE ABUNDANCE WHEEL

Once you've worked through these key questions and assigned a color to each of the five key areas of your business, it's time to move on to evaluating your life. My favorite exercise for evaluating the various areas of your life is what I call the "Life Abundance Wheel." Here are the 14 areas and what they each represent:

1. **Physical Environment:** This is where you live; your home or apartment. Your physical environment contributes to your overall wellbeing.
2. **Adventure and Fun:** Think of this as your "fun" life. These are activities and hobbies you enjoy.

3. **Career and Business:** This area is your career path and your business and/or chosen profession.

4. **Lifestyle:** This area has to do with the way you live out your life (eating habits, home location, dress, activities, values, etc.).

5. **Friends and Relationships:** Think about your friends, community involvement and social life.

6. **Finances:** This is your income, wealth, investments, retirement, cash flow, savings, and debt level.

7. **Giving Back:** This is your selfless service for the benefit of others.

8. **Personal Development:** This area has to do with what you do to learn or improve yourself emotionally and mentally.

9. **Family:** This is your married/single life, partnership, children, and extended family, as well as your level of involvement and commitment to those you consider family.

10. **Travel and Vacations:** Your vacations and getaways.

11. **Health and Wellness:** Everything you do to take care of yourself.

12. **Happiness:** How happy you feel.

13. **Marriage and Intimacy:** Your intimacy and relationship with your spouse or significant other.

14. **Spirituality:** As explained by PositivePsychology.com,* "spirituality can be defined broadly as a sense of connection to something higher than ourselves." You can find this through religion, meditation, community, volunteering, and so much more.

* Kelly Miller, BA, CAPP, "Science of Spirituality (+16 Ways to Become More Spiritual)," *PositivePsychology.com*, April 16, 2020, https://positivepsychology.com/science-of-spirituality/.

Taking a good, strong, purposeful look at these 14 areas and then developing a plan to optimize each area epitomizes living your life by design. The truth is, most entrepreneurs never take a thoughtful look at every area of their life. Instead, most focus the majority of their time and attention on building up only one area on the wheel: their Career and Business. This is the wrong approach.

When I first met Carter, he was working in his business all the time. He could not imagine allocating precious time and energy to anything other than making money. In fact, he didn't want to do anything else because he derived all of his pleasure from working. Although it is true that Carter absolutely loved what he was doing as a profession, it is also true that his family despised that it appeared Carter loved his work more than he loved them.

Carter was stuck in a classic oscillating pattern. He loved his work so much because he had never taken the time to create other life experiences that his family could enjoy *with him*. For Carter, it was all about creating new ideas and new things for his business. What Carter had not taken the time to learn is that there are many ways to create that don't involve having to forsake family. Once Carter discovered 3 Hours a Day, his life was revolutionized. He realized that what he loved so much was not necessarily his work, but the satisfaction he got out of creating. He learned that he could channel that same energy into other areas of his life and derive just as much or more in doing so.

When you begin to incorporate your being into the 14 life areas, you will go from living in black-and-white to living in vivid four-dimensional color. During this simple coaching exercise, I am going to guide you through the 14 different life areas. I want you to take an honest, heartfelt look at each one. Even if it seems to be an area that you are not very fond of, honestly ask yourself if your disdain is based on real experience or simply prejudicial judgment.

EXERCISE

Take a close and careful look at the Life Abundance Wheel below and consider each of the areas listed. Based on your satisfaction with each area, I want you to circle the appropriate number, rating it on a scale from one to five (one being not satisfied and five being most satisfied). You can find a link to download a copy of the Life Abundance Wheel in the Resources section or by going to 3HoursADay.com/bookresources.

As a reminder, you are rating *your current level of satisfaction* in each area, not your level of commitment to each area. This is an important distinction. For example, let's take the area of Spirituality.

If you don't have much of a spiritual life and spirituality is not important to you, then you could rank your level of satisfaction in this area very high, even if you have zero spirituality. Likewise, if you value spirituality and you feel that you are neglecting this area and not spending the time you would like here, then you might rank your level of satisfaction on the lower end of the scale.

Once you have circled the number pertaining to your current level of satisfaction in each area, you can clearly evaluate your entire life in terms of your level of overall satisfaction.

YOUR PERSONAL MEASURING STICK

In the previous chapter, we talked about the importance of knowing what you want. Now that you've rated your level of satisfaction with each area, I want you to write down your goals for each area. Use a separate sheet of paper for each area. You can write them out as bullet points, or however you wish. It is not important that you write your goals down in the order you wish each goal to happen. Instead, write down the goals you have as they come to mind, and be specific.

Try to keep most of your goals relatively short-term, i.e., within the next few years. You may write a few goals that are long-term, but keep these somewhat vague. Once you've done that, ask yourself, Why is this goal important to me?

Make sure to keep these pages! Your goals will likely need to be tweaked and upgraded over the years, and you'll also want to track your progress toward these goals.

You really never know where your career (or life) will take you. However, by having written goals, you will be able to gauge whether or not you are on the right track. Goal-setting acts as a measuring stick. Think about it: If you don't know where you are going, how will you know when you've arrived? How will you know when you've veered off the road?

All of these goals can be altered as you go along; however, they still must be written out as a foundation. If a marksman begins shooting without a target, how will he know when he has hit the bullseye? When goals are written or typed out, and perhaps pinned on the wall or on your desk, they serve as a constant reminder to the direction in which you are headed. The most successful people in the world write down their goals. Setting your goals will activate your subconscious mind, and it, too, will begin helping to accomplish your goals (even while you sleep).

Most importantly, *you must be absolutely convinced about the goal you set.* If you are not convinced about your goals, then your mind will never get on board to help you achieve them.

YOUR WORST ENEMY AND YOUR BEST FRIEND

I had an agent come to work for me once, and I asked him the question I ask anyone who is looking to join my real estate team: "How much do you want to make a month?" He pondered the question for a few moments and then shyly retorted, "$10,000 a month." At this I reeled my head back, wrinkled my forehead in amazement and said with vigor, "$10,000 a month!? That's a lot of money. Wouldn't $5,000 be all right?" He looked at me and then looked away. He thought about it for about two seconds. Now guess what happened during that two-second pause? Yep, he settled for less. "Well," he responded, "$5,000 wouldn't work, but $6,000 would be all right!" Two seconds was all it took for him to cut his pay by 40 percent. Mind you, I didn't give him a pay cut—he cut himself. All I did was sufficiently challenge him so that I could find out if his mind was on board with what he said he wanted. If your subconscious mind is not on board, you will never achieve your goals.

When it comes to getting what you want, who is your worst enemy? And who is your best friend and closest ally when it comes to achieving your goals? The obvious answer to both is YOU. Blaming others for your lack of success is a futile undertaking. Your own mind will develop every scheme imaginable to derail you and lead you to failure, and it generally doesn't need anyone else's help! You will sabotage your own success if you do not take the reins early on. You are the master of your mind; it is not the master of you.

Your brain will always look for the easy shortcut. When the goals that you set seem arduous, you will look for ways to ease the burden, typically by lowering your standards (reducing your goals). However, I have observed the flip side of this is also true. If you persevere even when the journey becomes unbearable, your mind will eventually get on board with your goals. Your mind will realize that this time, you are quite serious about achieving your objectives. At this point, both heaven and earth will begin to move to assist you in reaching your objectives. Your mind will not only get on board with what you are doing, but it will invent clever and exciting ways to make your journey easier and more successful.

If you have ever gone on a new diet, you have already seen this principle at work. Some years ago, I became convinced (actually, my wife Josie convinced me) that I needed to begin eating healthier. For me, that meant that I needed to incorporate fresh fruits and vegetables into my diet. But there was one big hurdle that I had to overcome: alas, I didn't like fruits and vegetables! The idea of sticking a leafy green substance into my mouth, having to chew repeatedly, and then having to swallow was not something I could fathom, so I came up with the clever solution of *blending*. I found that although I couldn't eat kale outright, I could blend it up into a smoothie and gulp it down almost before my tongue knew what hit it.

When I first started with the green drink, however, my mind was hard at work engineering my downfall. My brain would tell me things like, What in the heck are you doing now, son? You know you want a cheeseburger! I found that I constantly had to check and correct my subconscious mind: No, we are not doing a cheeseburger today, buddy! We are rollin' with that green drink! In time, however, my subconscious mind began to realize that I was quite serious about this new commitment. Eventually the dialogue from my subconscious mind began to sound like this: Wow dude, you're serious about this green thing, huh? Well, I guess it's not that bad after all. By my sixth month of healthy smoothies, my mind started screaming, Green drink, green drink! Gotta have that green drink!

My journey with the green drink illustrates how the mind works. When you originally move forward in any endeavor, your mind will seemingly attempt to sabotage your efforts to achieve success. As you push forward and your mind ultimately becomes convinced that you are serious about succeeding this time, it will get on board with what you are doing. This will be key to following through with your goals.

●　●　●

Now that you have taken a purposeful look at your business and evaluated it from head to toe, it's time to make some upgrades. It's time to get your business into perfect homeostasis. It's time to balance your business.

CHAPTER 5

Step 3:
Balance Your Business

N ow that we've evaluated where your business is, balancing
your business is the next logical step. To balance your business, you will lean on the eight key business pillars. I know! It
sounds like a lot to work on, but the work is so worth the result.
You are going to once and for all be able to live your ultimate
dream life.

THE EIGHT PILLARS OF
YOUR BUSINESS

Your business sits atop eight critical pillars: mindset, activities,
people, systems, tools, money, accountability, and training. Once
you master these eight simple pillars, your business will be in a
position to operate with or without you. Understanding these
eight pillars and shoring them up in your company is a critical
step before you can begin to scrape your plate. I have witnessed
many business owners and entrepreneurs assign tasks to a new
hire without first having these eight pillars in place. Inevitably,

without these pillars, you will end up with many of the tasks that you delegated back on your plate. The eight pillars provide a structure and system to ensure that your company operates most efficiently and achieves the level of success you desire without you necessarily having to show up.

Let's take a look at each of the eight pillars.

Pillar 1: Mindset

I feel like it should go without saying that mindset is the most important pillar. Mindset is what I call the "keystone" pillar because it permeates through the other seven. It has been well documented that success in any endeavor is at least 80 percent mindset.[*†] As they say, "If you believe it, you can achieve it!" As it relates to mindset, it is important to understand how the mind works, the functionality of the subconscious and conscious mind, the ego, and so forth. When you take on a new endeavor, your subconscious mind follows three phases: resistance, acceptance, and assistance.

During the initial resistance phase, your mind fights against you as it resists change. Of course you are excited about adopting 3 Hours a Day and enjoying the resulting freedoms, but perhaps you are also a bit apprehensive about what the future may hold. That's only natural. Soon, your excitement will fade into the reality that you have to start generating leads and getting business, and the doubt sets in: Are you sure you want to commit to this? This is hard! Your mind will try to talk you out

---

* Stefan James, "The Difference Between Success and Failure? It's All About Your Mindset," *Forbes*, March 19, 2019, https://www.forbes.com/sites/forbesleadershipcollective/2019/03/19/the-difference-between-success-and-failure-its-all-about-your-mindset/?sh=667690d34319.
† Prominence Global, "11 Secrets of the Entrepreneur Mindset," Prominence Global, July 28, 2017, https://www.prominence.global/secret-entrepreneur-mindset/.

of it once it sees that big changes are on the horizon. During the acceptance phase, your mind will reluctantly go along with the plan. Oh well. I guess we have to make these dang calls to generate leads. The resistance fades into action. Finally, when your actions become habits in the assistance phase, your mind gets fully on board with your vision and empowers you to succeed: Come on, let's go! Gotta set some appointments today!

Only when one can master the mind and then use it to one's advantage is true and lasting progress possible. The more you are aware of this process, the faster you can get through it. Many books have been written on how to rewire your brain, and it is the overarching theme in all of my books. To help facilitate the most significant strides, you will want to begin by reading at least one key book per month. I promote a "book of the month" to the students in my free coaching club, because it may be difficult for you to know which books to read to best transform your mind. Some of the favorites among the group are *The Power of Your Subconscious Mind* by Joseph Murphy, *Letting Go* by David Hawkins, *Feel Free to Prosper* by Marilyn Jennet, and *Ask and it is Given* by Esther and Jerry Hicks. Knolly Coaching Club is sponsored, so there is no cost to you. To join and get a monthly book club update as well as a monthly masterclass, go to KnollyCoaching.com.

Pillar 2: Activities

As an entrepreneur, your typical workday is made up of tasks and to-dos, otherwise known as your activities. As you already know, all activities are not equal. Through my training and coaching practice and from personal experience, I have learned that when you really break down all of the activities that you personally do each day, only about 10 to 20 percent of them are what I call income-producing activities.

Income-producing activities are made up of cash creation and wealth creation activities. Cash creation activities bring short-term cash flow into your business so that you can adequately fund all areas of your operation. Wealth creation activities bring ongoing or recurring revenue and/or large cash payouts into your business. All other activities are simply administrative, organizational, or ancillary activities whose purpose is to support your income-producing activities.

For example, when you look at the five areas of your business, which we covered in the previous chapter, you will notice that only marketing and sales can be considered income-producing activities. Delivery, operations, and finance are simply supporting roles. Part of running a world-class business is knowing where to place your focus. Utilizing the 3 Hours a Day system will allow you to place all of your focus and time inside of your zone of genius, so that every single hour of your workday will be energized and fueled with your passion and purpose.

Busyness doesn't equal business. Working for the sake of being busy is for the gullible and serves only to feed the ego. It's time to move from egocentric to efficient by focusing on just two Big Picture Priorities, and delegating everything else.

Pillar 3: People

The next pillar is people, and along with systems and tools it makes up what we call leverage. Leverage is the golden secret that makes 3 Hours a Day possible and it all starts with partnering with the right people. Remember, nobody succeeds alone.

I know firsthand that delegating can be super scary at first. Most entrepreneurs don't relish the idea of hiring people, but once you hire the right people, you'll enjoy the freedom that delegation brings you. Delegation is automation. When you have the right people in the right positions, and provide the right leadership, things automatically get done. Perhaps you've had a bad experience hiring people in the past. It's time to move beyond your past experiences.

When my wife and I moved from Austin to Puerto Rico, we knew that we wanted to take our infrared sauna with us because it would be next to impossible to find one on the island. It's a fairly large cedarwood unit that comfortably seats two people and takes up one-third of the size of an average bedroom. Initially, I wrestled with this beast for about 30 minutes, attempting to disassemble the unit without bothering to look for the instructions. Bad idea. Once I pulled up the instructions, the task was relatively easy. It turns out that the large panels that make up the unit have to be removed in a precise, sequential order, step-by-step.

Most business owners and entrepreneurs try to hire without following the 3 Hours a Day blueprint. This book serves as your instruction manual. Over the next few chapters, you will learn exactly how to hire, who to hire, and how to train, as well as what you should be delegating to others.

Pillar 4: Systems

Effective systems are vital to the efficiency of your business and to your ability to maintain 3 Hours a Day. When I speak of systems, I simply mean the precise, step-by-step way in which you perform a task or do something. When you combine a group of tasks into a chronological order, this collectively becomes your system. Creating a systematic approach that governs how your business is run is the leverage piece that will allow you to scale fast without fear of implosion. I teach my coaching clients that you want to implement systems that are easily duplicatable and scalable. For example, I am currently building an organization of more than 42,000 real estate agents across all seven continents.

From day one, I created a methodology for achieving this goal by simply studying and implementing the best practices of others who have already achieved the level of success I aspire to. After studying what the most successful folks in my field have done, I created my own system that is easy for my team members to adopt and duplicate.

Maybe it's time to take another look at your organization and what systems you have in place. If you are not a systems person (SC or CS on the DISC scale, or a steel on the Wealth Dynamics scale), you can hire a person to create and implement your systems for you. Or, better yet, adopt someone else's amazing system by licensing it from them and/or paying them to implement a similar system for your business.

When adopting or creating a system, always begin with the end in mind. Make sure that the system you implement is one that will not have to be drastically revamped. I see too many entrepreneurs start out small, only to outgrow their systems and have to start over from scratch in a few years. Map out exactly where you expect your business to be in 10 years and create a system *now* that will support your business of the future. If you don't know how to create a system, don't worry. In Step 5, I'm going to teach you how to create a stellar system for your organization. From there, you will simply need to adjust and tweak it slightly from time to time so that it remains relevant with your current needs.

Pillar 5: Tools

Having the right tools in your business will help you achieve the results you desire faster and with far less effort. Tools can come in the form of hardware, like machinery or equipment, and software, like websites and apps. Essentially, a tool can be anything you use to help you get the job done and reach your goals faster and more efficiently.

One of my favorite hobbies is baking. I bake anything from cakes to cookies, cobblers and the like. For me it is almost a form of therapy and stress release. As an amateur baker, I have learned all too well that the right tool can make all the difference in the world, not only on how my delicacies turned out, but also on how much easier it made the job. I spent many hours browsing through stores and picking up various gadgets to up my baking game. Having the right tools has been essential, not only in my hobbies, but especially in my business. In my real estate practice, my coaching/training business, and my software company, my team and I have enjoyed the use of incredible tools to help us get the job done more efficiently.

I've witnessed many entrepreneurs muddle along with outdated tools. Why? Usually it's because of laziness, time, or cost. They are too lazy or too busy to stay up to date on the latest tools and trends in their industry or they just don't have the money to spend due to poor sales and inadequate cash flow. It's important to understand that tools are an investment, not an expense. The right tools should help you earn a lot more money and save a lot of your precious time.

Pillar 6: Money

I named the sixth pillar "money," just because I like that name, but a more appropriate name would be "numbers." See how it's not as sexy? The money pillar is all about the financial numbers that make up your business. It's also about your money mindset. Money is a tool in your business and it also helps you keep score.

Now let me ask you a question: Who taught you what you currently know about money? Did they or do they have the kind of money you are looking to earn? If not, it's time to upgrade your teachers. As a child, I idolized my dad and he taught me many things, but making and keeping money was not one of them. Although he was a slick entrepreneur, he stayed at the hustler level his entire life. He never made the kind of money I desired to make. I don't say that with judgment, because whatever goals you have are yours and no one but you can judge you for your personal or business goals, but you should be learning from folks who have what you desire.

As a coach, I am frankly shocked by the level of financial illiteracy and the lack of acumen that many entrepreneurs display in this category. Before coming to me, many of my students haven't even bothered to take a cold, hard look at their finances. I have come to understand that, with most entrepreneurs, they are great at what they *do* but they are sorely deficient in many areas, such as financial stability, marketing, lead generation, and other critical areas that have the power to truly catapult their success.

It's fairly easy to come up with a spreadsheet to decide what your numbers should be in order to reach your goals. The easiest way to do this is simply to begin with the goal in mind and work backward from there. For example, let's say that you want to gross $100,000 per year. Depending on whether you have a service or a product, or both, you will then work out the numbers: How many widgets you need to sell, or the number of memberships you need to sell, or digital products you need to move in order to reach the goal. If you want to *net* $100,000, then you would of course add back in all of the operating expenses and overhead required to earn your $100,000.

STEP 3: BALANCE YOUR BUSINESS

Doing the Math: Examples

If you are a real estate agent, you would need to know the following data points in order to determine how many homes you need to sell each year to net your desired goal:

- Average sale price
- Your average commission percentage

Let's say you want to gross $100,000. If your average sale price is $550,000, and your average commission percentage on your side of the transaction is 3 percent, your average gross commission would be $16,500 per transaction. To determine this number, take the average sale price ($550,000) × the percentage split paid to you (0.03). Divide your gross income goal (in this case, $100,000) by the result ($16,500). This means you would need to sell roughly six properties per year to gross $100,000.

If you are a one-on-one coach, you need to know the following data points in order to determine how many monthly 1:1 coaching clients you need to have in order to gross $100,000:

- Your 1:1 monthly coaching fee
- Percentage split paid to you

If your goal is to gross $100,000, your coaching fee is $1,000 per month, and your split is 50/50, then you would need 17 active monthly 1:1 clients. To calculate this example, take your 1:1 monthly coaching fee ($1,000) and divide it by the percentage split paid to you (0.5): $1,000 × 50% = $500. Take that result and multiply it by 12 (the number of months in a year): $500 × 12 = $6,000 annually per client. Then take that result and divide it into your gross income goal: $100,000 / $6,000 = 16.6666667.

If you are an online marketer and you sell a digital product, you will need to know the following two data points in order to determine how many units of your product you need to sell each year to gross $100,000:

- Product price
- Your percentage split

If your product price is $697 and the percentage split paid to you is 100 percent, then you will need to sell 144 units in order to gross $100,000. That's 12 units per month. The math is product price × your percentage split ($697 × 1 = $697). Take the result and divide it into your gross income goal: $100,000 / $697 = 143.472023.

Don't be afraid of taking a deep dive into the numbers behind your operation—it's just math, and numbers don't lie. Of course, there are many other numbers in your business that need to be factored in, such as operating costs, overhead, labor costs, etc. that will have an impact on your net profit. In my businesses, I always aim to keep expenses low and income high. You want to work as efficiently as possible, and 3 Hours a Day will help you do just that.

Setting up an SRS to Cover Your Monthly Overhead

Another trick of mine is to have a secret revenue stream (SRS) that covers the cost of my monthly overhead. This can be a side product or service you offer, or an affiliate commission income, but my favorite strategy for this is continuity income. *Continuity income* is income that comes in month after month without you having to do a lot of (or any) additional work. Again, it has to be something that doesn't take up much of your time and can be almost completely run by your team or VA.

For example, if your monthly overhead is $5,000 per month, you could set up a monthly coaching program and charge $99 per month for folks to enroll. Once you have 50 students, your monthly overhead is paid and your other income streams are pure profit. Another great idea is to introduce your people to an amazing product you can endorse for an affiliate commission. To cover the monthly overhead in my businesses, I have Mentorship Masters (my real estate organization, which I operate on the eXp Realty platform). With Mentorship Masters, I generate residual and recurring income that covers all of my monthly overhead, and it only requires a few hours a week of my time because I have a VA that runs everything and a leadership team made up of volunteers. I also operate Knolly Coaching Club (my free monthly group coaching program for entrepreneurs and business leaders), which helps me— and my agents at Mentorship Masters—gain even more interested prospects.

Besides forecasting and reviewing your financial numbers, the money pillar is about improving your financial literacy. To learn the basics about money, check out one of my favorite authors, Richard J. Maybury. I highly recommend reading his work. You don't have to become a Rockefeller or Warren Buffett, you simply need to bone up on the basics of money and finance.

Pillar 7: Accountability

When I left home at 16, I doggedly vowed that I would never again let anyone tell me what to do. I wanted to be my own man. That belief has served me well in many of my endeavors throughout life, yet it has also been the root of my downfalls. Accountability is not about having someone else tell you what to do. Accountability is stating what it is that you desire and then having someone else review your stated goals against your actual outcomes. Don't be afraid of the word. *Accountability* simply means the ability to give an account.

When I am doing accountability coaching, we begin by reviewing what my clients' goals, dreams, and aspirations were for the week. I then ask whether they met, exceeded, or fell short of their goals. Their result will only be one of those three outcomes. If they fell short of their goal, I don't judge. I might ask a more pensive question like, "What do you feel got in the way of you reaching your goal?" I then ask, "What specific things are you going to do this week, such that, by doing those things, you will have either met or exceeded your goal by this time next week?"

The best way to introduce accountability into your business is to hire a coach. Most entrepreneurs don't want to hear that, and I don't relish the idea of forking over large checks either. But I never would have gotten even a smidgen as far as I have had it not been for my mentors and coaches, to whom I have paid considerable sums. (I have easily made back ten times my investments.) Today I have multiple coaches that I pay many thousands of dollars a month to, and I would not have it any other way.

Accountability is all about stating what it is that you want and then accounting for what you actually got. It is a calibration tactic, keeping you from getting too far off course, so that you will finish your year having solidly reached your goals. As such, weekly or biweekly accountability is far better than monthly or quarterly accountability. If you only have a monthly accountability call, you may have gotten so far off course during the month that it takes a good bit of work to get back on track. When you have a weekly or biweekly coaching call, you can adjust, tweak, and recalibrate on a weekly basis.

Pillar 8: Training

Becoming a world-class leader in your profession requires constant input from the right resources. Since you are reading this book, I'm guessing that you may already have dialed in on this pillar.

As the late great Jim Rohn taught us, you and I get paid in direct proportion to the perceived value that we bring to the marketplace. Therefore, the more valuable you become, the more money you will earn, and the less you will have to work to earn it. You should endeavor to become the most knowledgeable individual in your workspace. Of course, it's what you do with that knowledge that really counts, but the knowledge must be acquired first.

Since I am an avid reader, books happen to be my number one source for acquiring knowledge. However, it doesn't matter how you gain knowledge, so long as you're gaining it from the right sources. Be sure to spend at least two or three hours a week researching the latest tips, tricks, techniques, tactics, and tools in your industry. It's also wise to attend mastermind sessions, webinars, seminars, and/or Zoom calls hosted by top players in your field.

Because I enjoy acquiring knowledge as a form of habit and hobby, I tend to spend about an hour a day reading and/or gaining knowledge so that I can pass it along on my YouTube channel, to my Mentorship Masters, at my live events, on my podcast and TV show, and to my Knolly Coaching Club. Personally, I don't count this hour as part of my 3 Hours a Day. Oftentimes, I'll listen to an audiobook while working out, or doing things around the house, allowing me to accomplish multiple things at once.

Great training is what will keep you and your team operating more efficiently and will improve the work ethic and morale of your crew. Strive to be a lifelong learner and you will bring more value to yourself and those you serve.

Now that we've taken a good look at the eight pillars, which will help balance your business, let's move on to the fun part: delegation! It's time to scrape your plate.

CHAPTER 6

Step 4:
Delegate Your Business

ongratulations! You are halfway through the book! You already know what you have to do next: you have to let go.

That's right, the most dreaded thing for many entrepreneurs to do is let go of the reins. It is time for you to begin trusting others again. It's time for you to allow others to move your business forward under your careful tutelage. It is a scary thing to do at first, but in the end, the nightmare of pushing off the majority of your tasks onto others will become one of the most blissful dreams you have ever had. Delegation is the catalyst that brings about utopia in your business and personal life. In the meantime, I am here to guide you through the initial dread.

In order to enjoy 3 Hours a Day, you must delegate. You cannot keep all of the tasks on your side of the table and still hope to drastically cut down your workday. As they say, "something's gotta give," and in your case, that something is probably akin to 90 percent of your current daily tasks. First, you need to decide what you will keep on your plate and what you will scrape off of it. I'm going to make it easy: think of the things you love working on and scrape off the rest.

Remember when you were a kid and your mom told you that you had to eat everything on your plate? Maybe you ate the stuff you liked first and saved the stuff you hated for last. Then again, maybe you were brave and you ate the stuff you didn't like first. Well, you're not a kid anymore. I'm going to let you pick and choose what stays on your plate. Maybe you only want to eat the french fries. That's fine. Maybe you only want the chicken and mashed potatoes and you have no taste for the peas or the side salad. That's fine, too. And if you want to scrape your entire plate and only eat dessert, no problem!

In this next exercise we are going to determine what will stay on your plate and what will get scraped.

Decide What You Will Do and What You Will Delegate

There was a time that I was so overwhelmed in my real estate practice that I was at the point of either quitting the business or having a total meltdown. I knew that I had to do something drastic in order to avoid burnout. I was great at what I did and lots of clients wanted to work with me, but I just could not handle the workload. It was crushing me and bottlenecking my growth. So I came up with an idea.

I wasn't sure what I could possibly delegate to others, and since I've always been a control freak, I didn't really want to let go of anything. But I knew I had to in order to maintain my sanity. I got out a yellow notepad and I wrote down every single thing that I do in my business. (It was a sizable list of 46 different tasks, which included generating seller prospects, drawing up listing documents, obtaining the property survey, uploading photos to the multiple listing service, etc. If you're interested in seeing the whole list, you can find it in the Resources section at the end of this book, or at 3HoursADay.com/bookresources.)

Then, I came up with the idea to rate each task on a scale of one to five based on how much I enjoyed doing it. Many companies like Amazon, Yelp, and Google use a similar rating system.

Here's the scale I used:

1 = I hate it.
2 = I don't like it.
3 = I like it.
4 = I really like it.
5 = I love it.

After assigning the appropriate number to each task and reviewing my list for some time, I decided that I was only going to focus on tasks I rated a four or five, and that I would delegate everything else. This exercise changed my life more than anything else I have done inside my business.

Now, it's your turn. Write down every single task you can think of that needs to be performed in your business. For now, don't bother with organizing the list or trying to place the tasks in a chronological order. This is simply a brain dump. After you've written down every single task you can think of, it's time to rate them on a scale from one to five. On your plate you are going to keep the things that you really like or love, and the rest will be delegated!

Going Deeper

If you would like to further implement this exercise in both your business and personal life, simply write down *everything* you do over the next three days as you do it. (And I do mean everything.)

Here's an example:

- Woke up
- Personal hygiene
- Fed the dog
- Made coffee
- Tidied up the kitchen
- Made the bed
- Read emails
- Took a shower

And so on. . . .

This list will be helpful when you begin delegating things not only in your business but also in your personal life as well.

HIRING THE RIGHT PEOPLE TO DELEGATE TO

Now that you have the list of tasks you can delegate to others, it's time to hire people to take those tasks on.

After coaching tens of thousands of entrepreneurs, I have found that there are three core reasons you may have sucked at hiring people in the past: (1) you hired the wrong person for the job, (2) you did not have a clearly defined job description, or (3) you sucked at training. Let's take a look at each of these possible issues.

1: You Hired the Wrong Person.

In their eagerness to scrape their plate, most entrepreneurs hire someone exactly like them. This is the wrong move. For your first few hires, you should almost always hire the opposite of you.

You will hire someone exactly like you only when you are seeking to replace yourself and exit the business. For now, you are looking to simply scrape all of the tasks you don't like doing—or that aren't really the most income-producing activities—off to someone else. If you hire someone who is the exact same personality profile as you, and then delegate the things you don't like to do to that person, they will hate their job.

2: You Did Not Have a Clearly Defined Job Description (JD)

Even if you manage to hire someone who is the right personality profile fit for the job, you have to give them a clearly defined job description and they need to be working from a Team Operations Bible, which we will discuss further in the next chapter, so that they can understand the scope of their work, what your expectations are, and exactly how their job should be done.

Typically, there is a chasmic gap in communication. Since your hire will never become a mind reader, your expectations and their actions may never align. You may become disgruntled and take their job back, which leads to bitterness on both their part and yours. Next comes a breakdown of trust.

In this chapter, I will help you to craft a JD that is clear and concise.

3 HOURS A DAY

3: You Sucked at Training

Most of my coaching students run successful businesses. They are masters at their craft, but they really suck at conveying what it is that they do. They are terrible trainers, especially in 1:1 situations.

In his book *The E-Myth*, Michael Gerber explains how multimillion-dollar fast food and hospitality operations can operate proficiently by hiring the right personality profile for the job and implementing an amazing training system. For example, when someone goes to work at McDonald's, the manager or trainer doesn't just park them in front of the french fry machine and tell them to get to work. The trainer will walk them through every single step of the process: which buttons to push, when to push them, when and how to pour the frozen fries, when to drop the basket into the fryer, when to bring it back up again, how to shake the basket when the fries are done, how to dump the fries, how much salt to apply (and how to apply it), and so on.

This training technique goes from *I* to *We* to *They*. First, the manager will have the trainee simply watch as they do the job (I do it, you watch). Next, the trainee and the trainer will do it together (we do it). At this juncture, the trainer will do some of the steps and have the trainee do the other steps. Finally, when they feel the trainee is ready, the trainer will have the trainee complete the entire process by themselves under the close supervision of the trainer (they do it).

Since most entrepreneurs hire the wrong person and then fail to train them correctly, they end up with lackluster results to the detriment of their own success. You will finally achieve success when you begin hiring the right people and training them effectively.

By the way, you don't even have to have any of your systems documented before you hire help. In fact, it's best if you don't. As long as you train them correctly, you can have *them* document everything during the training process so that by the time they are finished training you will have your Team Operations Bible.

82

Why Are Your People *No Good*?

Many of my students come to me and say that employees they have hired in the past have mostly turned out to be *no good*. If you've had mostly duds in the past, there are only two possible reasons for this: (1) You made a bad hire or (2) you were a bad leader.

You Made a Bad Hire

In my real estate practice, I can't count how many properties I've listed where the previous tenant trashed it; the owner was always stuck doing renovations in order to sell. In almost every instance, the problem boils down to the fact that the owner failed to do the proper due diligence to secure the right tenant in the first place. They didn't do a background check, credit check, or prior rental history check. Had they paid $25, they could have gotten all of these reports done online, instantly. Plus, they could have charged their prospective tenant a $50 rental application fee to cover the cost of acquiring the report.

Later in this chapter, I'll teach you how to hire right in the first place so that this never happens to you.

You Were a Bad Trainer

The other more probable possibility as to why your employee was a dud is that you suck at training. Please don't take this personally; it is not a unique problem to you. When I say that you were a bad trainer, I do not mean that you are not good at leading your company. It goes without saying that you are probably pretty damn good at your core superpower, trade, and profession. But maybe you just suck at training others. Ensuring that your team is trained effectively is a key component of leadership.

The good news is that when you have the right people, systems, and tools in place, you don't have to become that great at training people. This is because good people have an internal governance and you will be providing them with good tools that will serve to make their job easier and good systems that will lead your people to exactly what they should be doing, when they should be doing it, and how they should be doing it.

In the music industry, a band leader typically has to pick the songs, write the songs, schedule the gigs, drive the van, wake up the band players, etc. An orchestra conductor, on the other hand, already has an elite group of world-class players who know exactly what they should be doing and when. The conductor has auditioned and hired the best people (the musicians), who have the system (the sheet music), and the perfect tools (the instruments). With the right people, combined with the right systems and tools, you can graduate from band leader to orchestra conductor.

WHO DO YOU HIRE?

Your very first hire should be administrative help. That is, an administrative assistant (Admin), who can handle all of the administrative tasks associated with your organization. Your Admin can also be trained to double as a lead coordinator and lead incubator, handling all the follow-up with your prospects, and assisting with marketing, social media, and inside sales. Many entrepreneurs don't hire an Admin because they feel that they cannot afford one. The truth is, you cannot afford *not* to have a good Admin person. This hire should be able to provide your clients and customers with superior service and make sure nothing falls through the cracks. This will result in higher client satisfaction and more referrals.

Your first hire will essentially be someone who can do the tasks you don't enjoy. They will do the tasks that you assigned a one, two, or three to during your exercise earlier in the chapter, and they will handle all or most of the non-income-producing activities in your business. Obviously, the goal here is to free you up to focus only on the things that you love to do and on the things that are creating immediate and future revenue for your company. You should also hire someone whose personality profile will typically be the opposite of yours, as previously discussed, so reviewing the person's personality test scores will be useful in making a decision.

Personality Profile Your New Hire

Have your potential hires take the DISC test and/or the Wealth Dynamics assessment in order to determine if they are the right fit for the position. Although the DISC personality profile is not the only area I take into account during the hiring process—it's afforded about 15 to 20 percent in my overall decision-making process—I do like to make sure that they are at least a personality match for the position. If you hire someone who is a proper match to the personality profile of the position, you are bound to yield better results and your hire should really enjoy their job, since it is a natural fit to their genius.

One trick to finding a great talent match is comparing a person's personality profile to that of a contact or current employee that already has the personality you are looking for. Having a profile to compare potential hires to will help you weed out candidates who aren't the right fit.

When hiring you can choose to hire either a VA, or, if you have a brick-and-mortar business, an in-house employee. There are pros and cons to either hire. If you have a brick-and-mortar location where customers and clients come to you in person, or a hands-on operation, where you need local staff in the field near the areas you serve, you will likely need to hire a staff member. If your business does not fall into this category, I highly recommend that you hire a VA. In fact, I own several companies and all of my team members are VAs. Some work from outside the United States, while others are stateside. Of course, there are advantages and disadvantages to hiring a completely virtual staff. For me, having a fully virtual team is an advantage, since I work better without the distraction of having people constantly around to interrupt my flow.

For entrepreneurs who are more hands-on, the disadvantage to running a virtual team is that your workers are not at a physical location where you can personally guide them. It can feel as if you are missing out on the camaraderie and synergy that is present when a team works together in close proximity. You will need to be very intentional about creating a sense of collaboration, so that your team members don't feel isolated. The easiest way to do this is to create a group sharing account (using Slack, Viber, WhatsApp, Workplace, etc.), where all of your team members can collaborate. You could also host a meeting each week with your team, as I do with my own.

Although I have worked almost exclusively from home since the age of 23, there have been a few stints where I rented an office space and had my team members file in at 9 a.m. and clock out at 5 p.m. What I liked the most about that setup was that I could call a team member into my office and debrief them right there in person, getting a sense of their energy and reading their body language. I could also easily call all of my sales team in to praise their work or to have a quick team meeting or brainstorm.

In today's landscape, working remotely is preferred by the majority of workers.* While it may feel that nothing can completely replace face-to-face collaboration, my team has been able to recreate that "in-person" feel on a virtual level and everyone on the team enjoys the flexibility that remote work provides.

For the most part, over the past eighteen years, my team has operated in a completely virtual model and I definitely would not have it any other way. I can oversee my team from anywhere in the world and easily maintain my 3 Hours a Day.

WHERE DO YOU FIND YOUR HIRES?

There are several places where you can find your team members. When hiring an in-house employee, I personally prefer to begin my search by utilizing my allied resources. *Allied resources* are companies that you are currently doing business with. Reach out to your key contacts at these businesses. Let them know exactly who you are looking for and send them a copy of your job description. When I ran a local real estate practice, all of

---

* Ashira Prossack, "5 Statistics Employers Need to Know About the Remote Workforce," *Forbes*, February 10, 2021, https://www.forbes.com/sites /ashiraprossack1/2021/02/10/5-statistics-employers-need-to-know-about-the -remote-workforce/?sh=7b065334655d.

my staff came by way of referral from my allied resources, and I bagged some spectacular individuals. The people that you do business with will oftentimes know of someone who is amazing and is looking for work.

I do not recommend that you hire what are known as full-time employees. Countless studies have proven that humans are incapable of remaining focused for eight hours straight* and, in my view, that model is outdated and should be condemned. Instead, hire part-time employees who can work between 10 and 30 hours a week at most. To find good employees, I've recruited folks who are newly retired and itching for *something to do*. In the real estate game, my first hire was Barbara. Barbara was 62 years young and was a retired executive assistant, previously employed at a local law firm. I found out about her by asking my allied resources if they knew of anyone that was a good fit for my JD. It turns out the managing broker at my firm knew Barbara from church and felt like she had the right skills for my Admin position. Barbara was with me for my entire real estate career! She was a most exceptional hire. After hiring Barbara, I added on Morris and Carolyn. They also stayed with me through my career in real estate. Both were discovered through allied resources.

Another option is to hire a VA. Back in the day, I was apprehensive about the idea of hiring a VA, as it would be someone who works from home, and could be located hundreds or even thousands of miles away. Back then I felt like I needed someone that I could communicate with face-to-face. But times are changing.

---

* Elizabeth Escar, "How Many Hours a Day Can a Human Actually Work? (What Science Recommends!)," *Iris Reading*, July 16, 2022, https://irisreading.com/how-many-hours-a-day-can-a-human-actually-work-what-science-recommends/#:~:text=But%20have%20you%20ever%20wondered,productive%20hours%20in%20a%20day.

In 2009, I shut down my office and sent my three Admins home. They continued to work for me in a virtual capacity. The idea was difficult for me to embrace. However, my Admins loved it. There are obvious pros and cons to this approach, but for me the pros have far outweighed the cons. Then, in 2013, my good friend Daniel Ramsey convinced me to bite the bullet and hire my first overseas VA. Daniel owns and operates MyOutdesk, one of the largest virtual assistant companies for professionals in a variety of industries. I had known Daniel for years, and we reconnected at a convention where his company had a booth. I told him what I was doing as far as my speaking engagements, touring, etc. and that we needed to hire a director of support for my software company, MoreSolds, since my current director had recently retired. "Dude, you need to hire one of our overseas VAs," Daniel told me quite convincingly. I told Daniel I felt like I needed to have someone local. After patiently listening to all my self-limiting beliefs, Daniel sat me down in front of a computer registration screen in their booth and said, "Dude. Hire one of our VAs and let's get you onto success." After a little additional coaxing from my wife, I apprehensively signed up. Hiring someone to work virtually from the Philippines was something I had never done before or seriously considered—and I've hired lots of people over the past 30 years. I decided to give it a try. After all, I thought, it's month-to-month and I can cancel anytime. I might as well give it a shot.

Expanding my horizons overseas for my staffing needs has been a game changer. Truthfully, it has been the best leverage move I have ever made, and it has completely freed me up to flourish because I am able to focus on what I love doing (teaching, writing, developing, training, mentoring, traveling, etc.). In fact, within six months of hiring my first VA, I had a team of three full-time overseas VAs!

Whether you hire a VA or an in-house Admin to handle your administrative duties, as a rule of thumb, I don't recommend that you hire them for more than 20 hours a week until you are generating a steady income or have created a recurring revenue stream that will monetize your hire. Instead, I would suggest you start by hiring someone who works for you 10 to 15 hours each week.

WRITING A GOOD JD IS CRITICAL

In January of this past year, my wife and I were hanging out with our good friends Nichole and Kimball at their vacation home in Bradenton, Florida. Nichole is a successful serial entrepreneur who owns several businesses with a combined income of more than $500,000 per year. She was having difficulty hiring the right person at one of her companies, so I asked if I could take a look at her JD. Wow. It was about five pages long, and even with my advanced qualifications I would have been intimidated to apply for that position! How you word your JD makes a world of difference. I was able to offer a Nichole a short business healing session, showing her a better way to formulate the document.

Oftentimes, business owners put together JDs that are far too comprehensive. I completely understand that you want to hire the perfect individual and you want to make sure that only the best candidates apply, but this can also backfire and overwhelm potential candidates, causing you to miss out on some great hiring possibilities. Having a JD that is robust and extremely comprehensive may also inspire your candidates to request a higher pay scale for the job.

While there *are* some specific things that you want to be assured your new hire knows, when you hire the right profile, they will easily be able to adapt and learn a variety of skills that they may not currently possess. Accordingly, you are hiring more for the personality profile of the position and the aptitude of the individual than you are for their current skill set. Great hires are made up of a combination of acumen, aptitude, capacity, character, personality profile, and skill. With amazing training and great leadership, they can be molded and shaped into exactly what you need them to be.

In the next chapter, we will go over the groundwork for creating your Team Operations Bible, a document that will allow almost anyone to step into a role and do the tasks you need done, so long as they have the correct profile for it. By documenting the systems that they will utilize in your business, your Team Operations Bible will chart the course for all of their activities. Therefore, if you can find someone who fits the profile and has good moral fiber, strong character, and a good amount of business skill, you should be good to go. You've got a clean slate to mentor and train someone into what you desire in an employee.

So, how do you create a good JD that is simple and effective? I have the perfect recipe for you. Here is the format you will follow:

1. **About the company**
   Here you will write out one or two sentences about your company.

2. **About the position**
   This should be three sentences maximum describing the position.

3. **Main responsibilities for the position**
   Bullet point the main responsibilities for the position.

4. **Job content**

   Here you can bullet point a few items, like if the position will be remote or if they will report to a main office, expected office hours, etc.

5. **Knowledge, skills, experience needed, and desired attributes**

   This will be a list of the knowledge, skills, and experience essential to the position.

6. **Proficient skills highly desired**

   This will be a list of skills that are highly desired but not necessary because you can train them on these items if needed. If potential candidates do in fact possess these skills, they will likely be looked upon more favorably, but it isn't imperative that they possess these skills up front.

7. **Goal/expectation**

   State the overall goal that you desire for this hire.

8. **Compensation**

   Place your compensation offer here.

9. **Term**

   Here you can place the term (time limit) of employment. I prefer to initially hire team members for a 100-day trial period and then reevaluate at that point in time. This gives me a long enough window to see if the hire is a good fit. If they aren't a good fit for me or they don't see the job as a good fit for them, their term simply expires and there are no hard feelings since a 100-day term was agreed upon up front.

Here's an example of a JD using this format:

Administrative Assistant – Job Description

About the company:
Knolly Training Company was founded by bestselling author, international speaker, and thought leader Knolly Williams. Our mission is to help entrepreneurs quadruple their income while working just 3 Hours a Day.

Our team administrative assistant will be responsible for ensuring that all administrative aspects are completed in a timely manner and per our system.

Administrative duties:
- Compile, edit, and use the Team Operations Manual that documents all systems and standards.
- Develop and implement systems for clients and prospects, lead generation, contact database management, and provide front- and back-end office support.
- Ensure that all systems and processes run efficiently, making revisions as needed.
- Answer and route all phone calls and incoming communiques.
- Coordinate the purchase, installation, and maintenance of all equipment and software.
- Develop and maintain the team virtual filing systems (clients, contracts, proposals, legal, correspondence, etc.) and computer databases.
- Complete weekly and monthly reports.
- Serve as initial point of contact in handling prospect and client inquiries and complaints.

- Responsible for all financial systems. This includes maintaining the books, paying the bills, handling payroll, ensuring the collection of commissions, maintaining the budget, and generating financial reports. Responsible for the accuracy and timelines of all financial information.

Additional duties include:
- Serve as key relationship for all contacts, prospects, and clients
- Conduct initial phone consultation with intake sheet
- Responsible for timely and consistent follow-up on all leads
- Draft sales documents and coaching contracts
- Schedule virtual meetings with potential clients
- Make weekly calls to clients and prospects
- Coordinate speaking engagements and podcast appearances for Knolly
- Additional and various tasks as needed

Knowledge, skills, experience needed, and desired attributes:
- Proficient computer skills
- Excellent phone skills
- Good people skills
- Friendly personality
- Attention to detail
- Ability to manage and lead others
- Ability to design and implement efficient systems
- Works well with little-to-no supervision
- Trustworthy
- Task oriented

- Results-driven
- Ability to prioritize
- Excellent written and verbal communication skills
- Internet savvy

Proficient skills in the following are highly desired:
- MLS system
- DocuSign
- Excel, Word, PowerPoint
- Google Suite
- Excellent and fast computer navigating skills
- Great management skills

Job Context:
- You will work remotely, from home. Schedule is 30 hours a week.

Goal/Expectation
- Your goal is to ensure that the office runs like a well-oiled machine—clean, efficient, and free of chaos.

Compensation
- This position pays an estimated $25,000 to $42,000 per year (based on the sales goals we project for this position).

Term:
- We will begin with a 100-day initial evaluation term. At the end of the 100 days, we will mutually evaluate each other and decide if we can continue the working relationship.

To download an editable version of this JD, go to 3HoursADay.com/bookresources.

Five Compensation Models for Your Admin

You can compensate your Admin in one of five ways. There are other models for how to pay your Admin, but these are the most widely used. If you are not utilizing an overseas VA, you will need to factor an additional 15 percent or more to these rates to cover your employer's portion of federal income taxes, plus additional expenses if health insurance is required. Check with your CPA or financial advisor.

1. Overseas VA: Pay per hour, 20 to 30 hours per week. Rate is typically $5 to $8 per hour to start.
2. Hourly: $15 to $30 per hour, or more depending on your market area.
3. Salary only: monthly salary of $1,800 to $4,000 (part-time) depending on the hours they work and the going rate in your field.
4. Base salary plus bonus: pay an Admin a flat monthly fee, say $1,500 per month (full-time) PLUS a bonus for client signings or a commission on sales.
5. Commission only: pay an Admin a fee per sale depending on the volume of sales per month and the specific duties they will be performing.

• • •

At this point you have figured out what you are going to delegate and you have taken a good look at *who* you will need to delegate to. Now let's take a look at systematizing your business. Don't sweat it—YOU are not going to do this; your new hire will! In the next chapter, I'll show you how.

CHAPTER 7

Step 5:
Systematize Your Business

You've come a long way, baby! You have honed your superpower, evaluated, balanced, and delegated your business. Now it's time to organize it all, by systematizing your business.

Large factories, warehouses, and even fast-food restaurants bring in millions of dollars in income while hiring a workforce primarily made up of unskilled laborers. They do this by making their operation plug and play. Not having your business completely systematized leads to you paying a lot more of your income to your employees and it leads to an inefficient operation. The bottom line is, your daily operations will cost a lot more time and money when your business is not systematized.

In Chapter 5, I shared that a system is the precise, step-by-step way in which you perform a task or do something. When you organize a group of tasks and write out the steps required for each task, this collectively becomes your business operating system. Once you have your business operating system in place and your team implementing that system, your business has become systematized, and you will be able to grow and scale your business more quickly.

In this chapter, I'm going to share with you a very easy method for systematizing your business . . . and you won't even have to do the work! But first, I want to make sure you avoid a big trap.

A BIG TRAP: THINKING YOU CAN DO IT ALL

A lot of the clients that I train and coach have a big problem with delegating. They believe the old adage, "If you want something done right, you have to do it yourself." For most entrepreneurs, however, this misnomer falls flat, since many of them are not very organized and don't tend to think or act systematically. The more appropriate truth is, "If you want something done at all, then you must hire others to do it!"

You need to understand where you are weakest and partner with people who are strong in those areas. So, how do you understand where you are weak? Usually, your weaknesses will manifest themselves as the things you are avoiding, the things you aren't particularly good at, or the things you simply don't enjoy doing. However, a simpler and more accurate way to understand your weaknesses is through the DISC personality profile test or the Wealth Dynamics test as we discussed in Chapter 2. By taking these simple online assessments, you will quickly see where your strengths and weaknesses lie. If you simply partner with others who are strong in the areas where you are weak, you will enjoy your greatest potential for success. For a free online assessment, go to my website at 3HoursADay.com /bookresources, where I provide links to my favorite free sites.

I come across entrepreneurs all the time who talk about how they are working on their weaknesses. "Well, Knolly, I'm not very organized, but I've been working on it!" Do you think the president of the United States is very organized? If not, do you think the president is working on becoming better at being organized? Probably not. Rather than waste your time working on the areas where you are not naturally strong, why not just build upon your strengths and partner with others who are strong in the areas where you are weak?

Don't get me wrong: You already know that I am a lifelong learner. I am huge on encouraging my coaching clients to become more self-aware, to constantly improve themselves. However, once you have proven without a shadow of a doubt that you are lacking in a particular skill set why not gracefully move on? Why not focus your energy on becoming even more proficient in the areas where you already excel?

For example, I love to write. Not only do I enjoy writing, it comes naturally to me and I am constantly working to improve my writing skills. Yet, even if I didn't like to write, I could still be an author. All I would have to do is partner with someone who is a writer and simply share with them all of my ideas, letting them articulate those ideas in written form. I like to think that our relationships with others is like an old western town: You had one barber, one schoolteacher, one blacksmith, a shopkeeper who ran the general store, a diner, a druggist, one or two small hotels, and one or two saloons, etc. In town, everyone had their own unique trade. Outside of town, you had the farmers and ranchers, each with their own unique crops and livestock. People would often barter with each other and trade the goods that they had. In this way, everyone had everything and no one lacked anything.

If you are not a great public speaker, then sure you should work on becoming better at speaking in public. If you are not a great writer, then sure you should work on improving that skill.

But I don't recommend that you work on mastering something that is outside of your superpower. Work on mastering the areas where you are already good, and turn good to great and then great to even greater. Realize that not everyone is meant to be gifted in all areas.

For example, if you are really good with people then you should probably be spending a lot of time with people. Forget about the paperwork, being organized, or data entry. Just fill up your social calendar with events, lunches, and meetups; and fill up your business calendar with appointments. Get in front of as many people as you possibly can each week and watch your business flourish. Then, simply hire others to handle the tidal wave of new business while you are out playing.

If you are a wiz with spreadsheets and paperwork but don't really enjoy being around people, then spend your time in the office running a revolutionary business practice with you in the control room pushing the buttons. While you are behind the scenes overseeing the organization, you can simply hire someone who is a people person to go out and do all of your company presentations. You'll be raking in the business!

Years ago I had a conversation with Chris Rios, an agent in my previous real estate office. In his former life, Chris was a master telemarketer at the very top of his game. When he transitioned into real estate, Chris decided from the very beginning that he would be a listing specialist, and he began making calls in the mornings and going on listing appointments in the afternoons. But Chris quickly figured out that he could actually generate more business if he did not have to go out on appointments. Since he is great on the phone, he wanted to spend his time doing nothing but prospecting. His solution? He simply partnered with someone who loves going out and doing presentations, but didn't want to be bothered with prospecting. It's a win-win relationship.

No matter where your strengths lie, you can succeed in your chosen field, but you must partner with others who are strong in the areas where you are weak.

DON'T WAIT UNTIL IT'S PERFECT!

I recently had the privilege of coaching Dawn Davis. Dawn is a perfectionist who suffers from analysis paralysis. Last year she earned $150,000, but she knows she should be earning closer to $500,000. Why isn't her income commensurate with her capability? It's because she has always had to ensure that everything was perfect and neatly in place before she felt comfortable moving forward into her greatness.

After a good bit of coaching, we discovered that Dawn's core issue was trust. Her trust issues ran so deep that they were actually handicapping the growth of her business. Someone had betrayed her trust at an early age and the cycle continued to repeat itself throughout her life. After that experience, Dawn came to the conclusion that if she wanted anything done, she had to do it herself, and it had to be perfect. Because she was unwilling to scrape anything off of her plate, overwhelm had crept in and her business was completely stifled and unable to grow.

Again, I find many of my coaching clients fall into this trap. They know they need help but they are afraid to let go. Even when they realize that they absolutely have to let go in order to avoid meltdown, they still believe that they need to have everything perfect before they can begin turning pieces of their job over to others. Nothing could be further from productive.

SYSTEMIZE THROUGH DELEGATION

The first thing you are going to delegate to your new hire is the systematization of your business. In theory, it might seem to make more sense to systematize your business *before* you delegate it, but in the real world that strategy doesn't really work that well. I've coached enough entrepreneurs to know that this is the part they absolutely flunk out on, because it just isn't in their wheelhouse. Forcing yourself to systematize your business before you delegate is asking you to do something that is, in most cases, outside of your zone of genius.

Following the model we discussed in the previous chapter, your first hire should be a whiz at organization. Therefore, you will be delegating the task of getting organized to someone who is far more capable than you. Within the first 100 days of their employment, this person will be responsible for creating your Team Operations Bible (TOB). This document will serve to systematize your business in such a fashion that any new hire should be able to pick up the baton, should one of your employees drop out of the race. Once you have your TOB in place, if an employee is absent for whatever reason, you should be able to quickly fill their position temporarily or permanently and rapidly get your new hire up to speed. Of course, to help mitigate employee turnover, make sure to hire correctly to begin with. We covered how to do that in the previous Chapter. Your TOB serves as the training manual and reference guide for your organization.

Next I'll cover the step-by-step instructions for systematizing your business and creating your TOB.

ORGANIZING DAILY TASKS

The first step for your Admin will be to take the entire list of tasks you wrote out in the previous chapter and organize them in chronological order as best they can, with your help. To do this, they will take a look at each and every task and look at when in the process it should be completed. This can be done on a whiteboard, using an app or software, or on paper. Next, your Admin will move the tasks around until they determine the best possible flow. I recommend they label the tasks in steps (e.g., Step 1, Step 2, Step 3, etc.).

If they don't understand the operation well enough to do this, or if they haven't been with the company very long, you or someone on your team can sit down with them in person or via video conference and help them learn more about the overall business so that they can organize the tasks accurately. Record the meeting for future training and ask your Admin to take meticulous notes.

The Psychology Behind the Task

It is important that your teammates understand the psychology and principle behind the task they are being asked to perform, so that they understand the reason *why* this task is important. The more folks understand why they are being asked to do something (and how each task fits in the grand scheme), the more worthwhile their job will feel, and the more satisfaction they will derive from doing it.

Bear in mind that your TOB may need to be tweaked from time to time, and that's to be expected. Your Admin will simply follow the instructions in this chapter to create a revised one-sheet for any of the procedures in your operation that change, or they can simply edit the document and accompanying video. Then, they can just insert the revised one-sheet into your TOB.

This next part is the meat of your TOB. Your Admin will be creating what I call a one-sheet for each task or step in the process. The format of each one-sheet should be: (1) title, (2) summary, and (3) instructions. Each of these one-sheets will collectively make up your TOB. To do this, your Admin will write out a summary in one or two simple and matter-of-fact sentences that describe the step, and then will type out a full-length, instructional step-by-step one-sheet for each task.

Your Admin should be detailed and should not leave any steps out, even if they seem obvious. For example, if one of the tasks involves logging into a website, they will need to document which website to visit, how to log in, what to click on next, etc. Each task should be descriptive enough so that almost anyone who joins the organization will be able to pick up the document and follow the instructions. Your Admin can also include any training videos they used to learn the task. Once they finish the TOB, simply use the chronological list of tasks that you originally compiled as the table of contents.

Record Videos

Once all of your one-sheets are created, record a step-by-step video for each document with you, your Admin, or with whoever handles that task performing the steps as they are laid out. This may seem a bit clunky and cumbersome, and it can be, but it is essential to creating a comprehensive TOB. Making new instructional videos that follow the format of the one-sheets may seem repetitive if you already have previously created videos. However, your former videos may not be very succinct. What you need now is a video that matches verbatim each step-by-step one-sheet. I like to add a link to the video just below the title on the one-sheet. I also like to indicate the length of the instructional video (in parenthesis), so that I can set the expectation of the viewer.

When recording, don't worry about getting it perfect. The videos can always be edited to remove any blunders. To record these, you can use your smartphone, or you can use an online video capture software like Loom or Camtasia.

Here are a few examples of instructional one-sheets I have created specifically for my real estate practice. Use these to guide you toward creating yours.

EXAMPLE 1:
Add Property to Knolly's Facebook Page

CLICK HERE for a TRAINING VIDEO on How to ADD a Listing to Knolly's Facebook Page (3 min.):

1. Log into Facebook.
2. Add JUST LISTED or JUST SOLD headline.
3. Add the price and property address.
4. Paste the internet remarks from MLS.
5. Paste the LINK to the property from Knolly's site: KnollyTeam.com.

6. Upload the photos of the listing.
7. Post.

EXAMPLE 2:
Creating a New Listing in Skyslope

CLICK HERE for a TRAINING VIDEO on How to Create a New Listing in SkySlope (2 min.):

1. Log into Skyslope.
2. Select Create Listing then click Enter the Listing.
3. Key in the property address (as you begin typing, the smartsearch will attempt to find the property).
4. Click Let's Go.
5. Select This is My Listing.
6. Select Texas Residential Listing > Next Question.
7. Enter or confirm price > Next Question.
8. Listing Commission: 3.5% | Sales Commission 2.5% > Next Question.
9. Input the listing date and expiration date (from the listing agreement) > Next Question.
10. Confirm year built > Next Question.
11. Source of deal: select appropriate choice from the pull-down menu > Next Question.
12. Input client name(s).
13. Click CREATE MY LISTING.

Congratulations, once all your one-sheets are completed, you have now systematized your business! It's really that simple. Next, we will design your 3 Hours a Day.

CHAPTER 8

Step 6:
Design Your 3 Hours a Day

Wow! You've made it a long way. By now you have already honed your superpower, evaluated your business, balanced your business, delegated your business, and organized your business. Now it's time to design your perfect 3 Hours a Day.

There are three different levels of 3 Hours a Day: beginner, intermediate, and advanced.

- **Beginner:** Start by carving out 3 Hours a Day WITHIN your current workday. Focus on only doing income-producing activities during this three-hour timebox. You may still be working eight to ten hours a day at this point, and that's okay.
- **Intermediate:** Delegate most/all of your non-income-producing activities to someone else, and cut your workday in half. You may still be working four to six hours a day at this point.
- **Advanced:** You are now ONLY focused on income-producing activities. Everything in your business is operating as a well-oiled machine and you are working three hours a day or less.

3 HOURS A DAY

3 Hours a Day is not all-or-nothing, nor is it one-size-fits-all. I have students who choose to only work three hours a day (or less). Others work six hours a day and incorporate my 3 Hours a Day methodology into their daily routine. Regardless, they are working far less and finally enjoying the fruits of their labor.

YOUR TWO BIG PICTURE PRIORITIES

In the grand scheme of things—outside of supply chain issues—there are only two problems that any business owner will have to solve: not having enough money, and not having enough time. If you can find solutions to these problems, then you will have a thriving business for decades to come. In this chapter, I will help you solve both problems and in doing so, will also help you fashion your dream schedule.

If you have an amazing product or service, but you don't have enough clients or customers to generate the consistent cash flow you need to thrive, then you have a money problem. This problem is solved by consistent daily lead generation. When you generate more leads, you create more clients and customers, which solves your money problem. Once you are generating so much business that you can't handle it all, you have now created a new problem: not enough time. This problem is solved by leverage. When you bring on people, systems, and tools, and use them to systematize and automate your business, you are able to create a business that runs with or without you. This solves your time problem.

Paradoxically, many entrepreneurs find themselves in a vicious loop by cycling back and forth between these two problems. Because they are truly great at what they do, word about them spreads fast and they generate so much business that they can't keep up with it all. Consequently, they take their foot off the lead generation pedal and stop generating new business. Within a few months their pipeline of revenue dries up and they have to go back to generating additional business only to become overwhelmed again. We call this the feast-or-famine cycle. When you focus on your two Big Picture Priorities during your 3 Hours a Day, you will avoid this conundrum.

Ultimately, you will want to focus primarily on two Big Picture Priorities and have someone else handle everything else. Those priorities will vary depending on what your business needs. For example, if you are not yet reaching your financial goals and/or your cash flow isn't steady, your two Big Picture Priorities will likely be centered around generating leads and closing clients, with an emphasis on building a steady pipeline. This means leads and sales will be your primary area of focus.

Your Sales Process

Depending upon your profession, your sales process will vary. For example, if you are a real estate agent, you will need to follow a three-step sales process. After generating the lead:

1. You have to sell the prospect on setting an appointment with you.
2. At the appointment, you have to sell the prospect on hiring you.
3. You have to sell the house in order to get paid.

Yes! You have to make three sales *before* you get paid!

3 HOURS A DAY

> If you are a chiropractor or a coach, you will follow a two-step sales process:
>
> 1. You have to sell the prospect on setting an appointment with you.
> 2. At the appointment, you have to sell the prospect on hiring you.
>
> If you are an online marketer, you will also follow a two-step sales process as follows:
>
> 1. You have to convince the prospect to click on your offer, which will land them on your sales funnel.
> 2. You have to sell the prospect on ordering your product, along with any upsells.

If you are already reaching your financial goals and are over-whelmed by the sheer volume of work, the right leverage will solve your problem. In this case, your two Big Picture Priorities will likely be focused on branding and leadership. You need more leverage with an emphasis on scaling your business to break through to new financial goals. Let's explore what some of these Big Picture Priorities might be in your business.

BIG PICTURE PRIORITY 1: LEAD GENERATION

When your biggest problem is money, you must be primarily focused on growing your business, and to do this I want you to focus on a structured system for generating leads. Before you go generating a ton of leads and get yourself all worked up and entangled in another cycle, be sure that you have already completed Steps 1 through 5 of 3 Hours a Day, which I laid out in Chapters 3 through 7. This will ensure that you have the infrastructure in place to handle the leads that you will be generating.

Lead Generation Activities

In ancient times, our forefathers were hunter-gatherers. Back then, people migrated with their food source, and hunting for their next meal was not an optional exercise. No matter how scarce the surrounding food supply seemed, our ancestors would relentlessly chase their prey until they achieved success. For them, failure meant starvation and death. So, when the food supply was abundant, they stockpiled, carefully preserved, and stored the surplus. In good times and bad, they never took their eye off the ball.

In our day and age, daily lead generation includes things like making phone calls to our database of past clients and prospects, sending out e-newsletters, being active and purposeful on social media, creating online advertising and promoting videos about our products/services, initiating AI-based systems, sending out quarterly postcards, canvassing areas on foot, advertising, marketing, and utilizing our database of fans and loyal customers to help promote our products or services.

In order to receive a paycheck, you have to make a sale. In order to make a sale, you have to have a client or customer. And in order to have a client or customer, you have to start off with a prospect. In order to have a prospect, you have to lead generate. For maximum efficacy when generating leads, you should be focused on what I call the "three lead buckets," which are (1) your SOI, (2) your farm (geographic or demographic), and (3) your niche.

Your SOI includes the folks that already know you or know of you. These are the people who are in your database, and from

111

my experience, when marketed to consistently, they typically are your biggest bucket. Your farm is a geographic, demographic, or digital area that you choose to dominate to gain a loyal following of clients and customers. Your niche is your specificity or specialization. Think about a niche as your specific area of expertise, which sets you apart from all the competition in your industry.

It may help to think about the three lead generation buckets as the three legs of a stool. Suppose you wanted to sit on a heavy duty three-legged stool. Your weight is distributed across the three legs equally. What would happen, though, if you took one of those legs off and tried to sit on it? The stool simply would not support you. What if you took two of the legs off? You would end up flat on your back. Sadly, most entrepreneurs are trying to sit on a one-legged stool by focusing strictly on their SOI—and that one leg that they do have is busted and in disrepair.

Why Entrepreneurs Don't Prospect

There is a wide array of excuses that entrepreneurs provide for why they do not prospect regularly. No excuse is warranted or valid. Lead generation is a daily activity.

Lead generation is critical to your success. Here, I would like to address some of the most common excuses that I've heard for not prospecting. Let's examine them together:

EXCUSE 1: "I'm So Busy! I Just Can't Seem to Find the Time!"
Imagine our forefathers waking up and thinking, I have a lot of things to do today, so I guess I won't go out hunting. Feeding my family can wait.

In our businesses, we can easily become distracted by that which is urgent and forget about that which is truly important. Everyone and everything may seem to be vying for your attention, but nothing deserves it more than your lead generation time. The time you dedicate to lead generation should be anchored to your schedule and honored daily.

EXCUSE 2: "I've Tried to Carve Out Time but I Keep Getting Distracted."
Allowing yourself to become distracted means that you are not correctly protecting your scheduled time for lead generating. Be sure that everyone in your family and your office understands the importance of this activity. In ancient times, nothing was more important than hunting. This still holds true today.

Purposely protect your lead generation space by hanging a note on the door that says "LEAD GENERATING. PLEASE DO NOT DISTURB." Close the door if you can. Also, take any snacks, coffee, water, and other supplies with you into your lead generation bunker. Even the distraction of leaving your desk to fetch a drink of water or a coffee refill may prove fatal. If you are any less than supremely disciplined when taking short breaks, then you should be anchored to your desk until you have achieved your goal for the day (e.g., lead generate for 90 minutes, make 20 contacts, set two appointments, etc.).

EXCUSE 3: "I Just Can't Get in the Habit of Dedicating a Set Time to Lead Generate."
You absolutely *can* get into the habit of scheduling time for daily prospecting because you already do it

3 HOURS A DAY

now. In fact, you have learned to do this since the day
you were born. Do you go to sleep every night? That's
a scheduled activity. Do you brush your teeth, shower,
and get dressed every morning? Eat meals every day?
Each of those is a scheduled activity. When you worked
a nine-to-five job, did you go to the movies during your
work hours? Of course not, because you dedicated eight
hours for work and did personal activities during your
off-work hours! Even when you go to the movies, you are
scheduling two to three hours of undisturbed time. Trust
me, you've got this.

EXCUSE 4: "I Don't Know What to Say."
Knowing what to say is critical and oftentimes we fail to
lead generate because we either don't know what to say
or are afraid we will say the wrong thing. Knowing what
to say is a matter of training and learning your scripts.
Understanding human behavior and tapping into your
intuition is also critical. In his book *Exactly What to Say*,
Phil M. Jones helps you tackle this problem.

EXCUSE 5: "I Don't Know What to Do."
You have your schedule and plopped yourself down
at your desk promptly at 9 a.m. Now what? Obviously,
knowing what to do during your lead generation time is
very important.
     During your lead generation time, you should be:

1. Prospecting for new clients/customers (lead
   generation)
2. Following up on your existing leads (lead incubation)
3. Developing and implementing marketing plans

BIG PICTURE PRIORITY 2: SALES

Again, if your main problem is money, you will spend your mornings generating leads and spend your afternoons closing sales. You want to generate leads at the beginning of your day because that is when your energy and creative flow is most likely at its peak. To create more cash flow for yourself, you will also want to become a master at selling and handling objections. An *objection* is any resistance a prospect may have to purchasing your product or service, usually posed as a question. The question can be verbal or nonverbal.

What Is an Objection?

Think of some words that you would consider being synonymous with the word *objection*. What comes to mind? Typically we think of objections as *obstacles*.

What I want you to realize is that *an objection is not rejection*. An objection is an *opportunity*.

Let's say, for example, that you are talking to a prospect about purchasing your product or service and they throw out an objection such as "I like what you have to offer, but it's a bit more than I want to pay right now" or "What makes you think you can sell my house when my previous agent couldn't?" With these questions, what is the prospect really saying? I believe they are saying, "Look, I think you can probably solve my problem and I want to work with you. Can you please confirm for me that I am making the right decision?"

If the prospect did not want to explore the idea of purchasing your product, service, training course, etc., they would not throw out an objection in the first place, they would just say "no, thanks," and move on with their day. The prospect simply needs you to help convince them that they are making the right decision.

Think about the way you make big decisions. Before you swipe the card on that $800 purse, a flood of questions races through your mind. "What's your return policy?" "When did you say the newer designs are coming in?" "What if I find it for less somewhere else?"

Why do you ask this barrage of questions right before you make a big decision? We are programmed to be afraid to make mistakes. We throw up objections to protect ourselves. We want confirmation that we are making the right decision before we fully commit. We may also want to know where the escape hatch is (or whether or not there is one) before we jump on board. Once our objections are handled, we can feel safer about moving forward.

As a successful entrepreneur, when you handle objections effectively you are reaffirming to the prospect that they are making the right decision by doing business with you.

Over time, and with the right training, you will learn to handle objections masterfully.

The Four-Stage Lead Lifecycle

In sales, all leads have what I call a four-stage lead lifecycle: generate, capture, incubate, and convert.

Most entrepreneurs speak about and focus on just one stage in this process, lead generation. But trying to generate leads without capturing, incubating, and converting (lead follow-up) will not necessarily lead to clients, and will always lead to inferior results. Those who focus merely on Stage 1 will miss many a payday. Stages 2 through 4 are the stages that determine if a lead will live (and reward you monetarily along with the possibility of repeat business) or die (and reward you with nothing).

Stage 1: Lead Generate

We call this first stage "lead generation." This is the stage where the hook is baited and you are fishing for leads. Lead generation involves marketing, promotion, selling and a variety of other tactics required to generate a lead.

Stage 2: Lead Capture

We call this stage "lead capturing" or "lead receiving." During this stage you have the lead captured, but it is uncertain whether or not this lead will actually turn into a paycheck for you. Hard work and diligence is required in order to take the lead all the way to the pay window.

Stage 3: Lead Incubate

This is what I call the "nurturing" stage. As my mentor Rand Smith says, "in order for someone to work with you, the possibility of trust has to exist."

Think of this as the step where you are getting the lead to trust you. You are nursing the lead and trying to get them to see that working with you is a better choice than working without you. You are working to show them that you can be trusted. Sometimes the lead incubation process is quite lengthy. Other times, depending on the lead source, their timeline, your skill level, and contact frequency, it happens very naturally and quickly.

Stage 4: Lead Convert

Leads that are converted become clients or sales. In order to take a lead all the way to Stage 4, you typically have to connect with them at a subconscious and emotional level.

It is unfortunate that many entrepreneurs completely drop the ball when it comes to stages two and three. Many of the type A personalities (high Ds on the DISC profile) that I train try to take a lead from Stage 1 directly to Stage 4—generation straight to conversion. If the lead doesn't convert right away, they move on to the next one. Don't make this mistake. Stages two and three are where the magic happens. If you want to build your business to the highest level it can possibly be, you will have to get good and consistent at capturing and incubating your leads. You can easily double your business just by making sure your leads are captured and incubated. These leads can often turn into customers and clients months down the road. If you do not focus on these critical stages, then many of your potential sales (and paychecks) will simply fall through the cracks.

You'll be happy to know that you can delegate Steps 2 through 4 to your team members if they are highly trained and skilled at converting leads. (Yes, it truly is an art form.) You can also make use of drip email campaigns, funnels, and other systems to help you capture and incubate your leads. Plus, there are also some done-for-you solutions available.

Whether your appointments are live and in person or via phone or video conference, having direct connection with potential prospects and clients is crucial. The whole purpose of generating leads is to generate opportunities to close on the sale. If your product or service is digital, then you might be using various funnels or a sales team to automate this process, and if so all the better. You've now freed up even more time!

BIG PICTURE PRIORITY 3: BRANDING

So let's say you are generating a nonstop supply of leads, you have solved your money problem, and your business is booming. Now you face a second problem: not enough time to manage all that growth. When this happens, your Big Picture Priorities should be centered around growing your brand and leading your team. Once you have mastered lead generation and sales, and you are ready to scale, you can automate this process by hiring others to duplicate your success in these areas.

Simply put, your time problem is solved by leverage. In fact, you can scale your business to any level without having to work more than three hours a day once you master the leverage piece, have your Team Operations Bible in place, and everyone on your team is on the same page. You are now free to really let your superpower shine and become the brand ambassador for your company.

Building your brand is basically marketing (lead generation) on steroids. You will need to have someone on your team focus on generating promotional opportunities (or hire a publicity agency). This individual or company will help get you booked on podcasts, speaking events, cross promotions with other brands, etc. In my own business, I chose to work with 2 Market Media. They helped me to redefine my brand, have booked me on numerous podcasts, put together an amazing TV show, and they secured for me a major publishing deal with McGraw Hill, which lead to this book you are now reading. Plus, the coaching they have provided me along the way has been priceless.

The formula for marketing during your promotional opportunities is simple but very counterintuitive for most entrepreneurs including myself, because it involves giving a lot of value away for free in order to create the biggest list and the most sustained loyalty:

- **Step 1:** Provide value for FREE. Help others solve their biggest problem with your product or service. You can do this on a podcast, through an in-person or virtual training, YouTube videos, a monthly newsletter, blog, etc.
- **Step 2:** OFFER a FREE item of value or trial of your product or service. During your call to action (CTA), offer folks a free item of value (IOV). This can be a special report or download, a book, a training, Facebook group access, a free trial, etc. You could even provide a free consultation! It'll all depend on your particular business. Think of what would be most desirable to your ideal client and make it into a free offer. During this step you will capture the contact information of your prospects so that you can incubate and close them in due time.

BIG PICTURE PRIORITY 4: LEADERSHIP

Your fourth Big Picture Priority will be leadership: leading your team to the success you desire and deserve. As the conductor, everyone in your orchestra is following your lead and playing according to your acute direction. The speed of the leader is the speed of the group. Make it your job to learn as much as you can about becoming an effective leader.

Your team already has the playbook (your Team Operations Bible) and each member is aware of their role and their Success Goal. A Success Goal is a goal that clearly articulates the expectation of your team member. The purpose of having a Success Goal is to remind your team members of their goal and track their progress toward hitting them. Below you will find some examples of Success Goals. You will want to meet with your team regularly—consider a daily huddle or a weekly meeting—to promote synergy and to help keep everyone focused on the end result.

One concept that will keep the ball moving forward in your company is to create quarterly objectives. You will write down and disseminate the big goal(s) that you have for your team to implement that quarter, and then you will perform a review at the end of each quarter to see how the results achieved measured up to the goal(s).

Another great idea is to have your team members fill out a weekly tracker that states their Success Goal and shows you where they are in terms of meeting that goal. Have them send you their Success Goals worksheet and their results every Friday. You can also incorporate this process via a shared spreadsheet that they fill out weekly. This is really a psychological exercise that keeps your team members on pace and reminds them of your expectations on a weekly basis.

Here's a sample format for weekly or monthly Success Goals:

My JOB TITLE will have successfully fulfilled their role when they have consistently WEEKLY SUCCESS GOAL.

Here are some examples of Success Goals:

- My lead listing agent will have successfully fulfilled their role when they have consistently listed two homes per week.

- My buyer agent will have successfully fulfilled their role when they have consistently closed three homes per month.
- My team recruiter will have successfully fulfilled their role when they have consistently recruited two team members per week.
- My sales manager will have successfully fulfilled their role when they have consistently sold eight overnight celebrity toolkits per week and they have consistently booked me on two events per week (podcasts, virtual trainings, etc.).

Weekly Performance Review

Now that you have your Success Goals in place, you can begin conducting a 10-to-15-minute weekly review meeting with your top team members. During the weekly meeting, you will ask them if they met, exceeded, or fell short of their goal. If they met or exceeded their goal, you will want to provide adequate praise and appreciation. If they fell short of their goal, don't judge. Instead of asking "Why didn't you reach your goal?" ask "What specific things are you going to do this week such that by doing them you will have met or exceeded your goal by this time next week?" Let them come up with the solutions.

Those Who Report to You

You never want to have more than three people directly report to you, no matter how large your organization becomes. Even if your organization has thousands of members, for you, it should have the feel of a small team. When you have too many people reporting directly to you, it diminishes your bandwidth. Having a small team is really important to the success of your 3 Hours a

Day, because it means you can scale up while maintaining your ideal schedule. As your organization grows, your managers and supervisors will repeat the process of meeting with their team members. The managers under them will do the same, all the way down the line.

When utilizing your Team Operations Bible, quarterly success objectives, Team Member Success Goals, and weekly performance review with key members, coupled with your weekly team meeting or daily huddles, leading your team becomes extremely easy and reaching success becomes inevitable.

A DAY IN THE LIFE OF A SUCCESSFUL 3 HOURS A DAY ENTREPRENEUR

As you can see, if your main issue is money, you will need to focus on Big Picture Priorites 1 and 2. If your main issue is time, you will need to bring on leverage, while you focus on Big Picture Priorites 3 and 4. Now that you've learned how to find and work on your two Big Picture Priorities, let's see what a 3 Hours a Day schedule could look like for you:

6–7 A.M. | Personal Growth (meditation, reading, prayer)

Successful entrepreneurs are always expending positive energy. It is critical that you take time for yourself to refuel your inner person so that you don't run dry and burn out. Personal growth time allows you to fill back up and ignites your motivation by reminding you of your purpose.

7–8:30 A.M. | Personal Care

Find some time to exercise, eat a healthy breakfast, and dress for success before going off to your lead generation bunker! Personal care preps you for success and equips you with the physical energy to make it through the day.

If your main problem is money:

9–10:30 A.M. | Lead Generation/Prospecting

The successful 3 Hour a Day entrepreneur is first and foremost in the lead generation business. At this phase of your business growth, prospecting will consume the first part of your work day. During this critical time, you will be focused on three activities: (1) generating new leads, (2) following up on leads received, and (3) developing and implementing marketing plans.

If your main problem is time:

9–10:30 A.M. | Branding

At this point in your business growth, you have already delegated your basic lead generation and all administrative activities to someone else and you are now focused primarily on being an ambassador for your brand. This means filming YouTube videos, recording podcasts, writing books, blogging, and more. During this critical time, you will be focused on three activities: (1) creating mass awareness of your brand, (2) creating strategic alliances with other brands, and (3) developing and implementing branding strategies.

If your main problem is money:

10:30 A.M.–12 P.M. | Close Sales

Successful 3 Hour a Day entrepreneurs spend the second part of their day closing sales with prospective clients and prospects. This may involve going on appointments or phone sales, etc., depending on your profession.

If your main problem is time:

10:30 A.M.–12 P.M. | Leadership

Once you have someone on your team who is following up on your prospects and handling sales, you can spend the second part of your day leading your team. This may involve team meetings, huddles, and overseeing the five key areas and eight pillars of your operation, which we discussed in Chapters 4 and 5.

12 P.M. | OFF

• • •

In order to achieve success with your 3 Hours a Day routine, you will need to fix your two Big Picture Priorities to your calendar. I have learned from experience that if it's not on my schedule, it can easily get lost in the shuffle. Set it on your calendar as a hard and fast daily appointment, and don't break the routine.

CHAPTER 9

Step 7:
Quadruple Your Income with 3 Hours a Day

In this chapter, I want to introduce you to five classic ways to quadruple your income using 3 Hours a Day as your model. With this system you will not only be working less, but you will be earning a lot more as well. These five strategies are ultrasimple and easy to implement, but they are often forgotten because they require you to be purposeful.

1. DELEGATE YOUR BUSINESS

Releasing 90 percent of your workload frees up your mindshare so that you can work on your business, focusing only on the most income-producing activities. While the gift of cutting your workday by two-thirds is a huge blessing to you and your family, 3 Hours a Day also allows you to substantially increase your income because it allows you to focus on the Big Picture Priorities in your business.

Michael is one of my students who recently graduated from my four-day "3 Hours a Day" boot camp. Michael owns three successful businesses and he used to work *all the time*. By following the system you have learned in this book, Michael was able to drastically reduce the hours he works every day by focusing on his Big Picture Priorities and delegating everything else. Michael has been an entrepreneur for more than a decade, yet within a few months of implementing this system, he had his best sales month ever. Michael's story is not unique. The 3 Hours a Day movement is strong and thousands upon thousands of entrepreneurs are becoming liberated and experiencing ultimate freedom for the first time.

It may be counterintuitive to equate working less with earning more, yet this is the promise of 3 Hours a Day. That's because with 3 Hours a Day you aren't simply cutting your work hours; that would be detrimental for your business. Instead, you are adopting a success system that is long overdue, letting your carefully picked team handle tasks you don't enjoy doing and freeing up your mind to work on the truly important issues in your business.

Delegating tasks you don't enjoy or that aren't the most income-producing frees you up to work on the things in your business that both increase your cash flow and your wealth.

Your Limited Mindshare

One of the key benefits of delegating is that it frees up your mind so that it can focus on the Big Picture Priorities that will allow you to experience rapid growth and success.

The human mind is incredible. Even so, the mind has a limited capacity when it comes to focusing on multiple things at once. Just like the storage on your phone or computer, there is a limit. Additionally, the mind lacks the ability to *prioritize* without proper guidance.

Typically, the ideas that lead to income creation are quite simple, but your brain isn't all that efficient. In truth, it takes the same amount of brain power to work on solving a $500 problem as it does to come up with a $10 million idea. That's why it is important for you to be very selective about what you allow your brain to focus on. Delegating 90 percent of the tasks you formerly had on your plate frees your mind to tackle the big problems your business faces.

2. INCREASE YOUR NUMBER OF CUSTOMERS

It should go without saying that building your clientele list will lead to building up your business. Increasing your number of customers or clients means that you will need to grow your audience and grow your list. This is why it is so important for you to make lead generation and/or branding one of your two Big Picture Priorities as I laid out in the previous chapter.

Here I want you to list 5 to 10 things that you can begin doing to grow your audience and build your list:

1. _____

2. _____

3. _____

4. _____

5. _____

6. _____

7. _____

8. _____

9. _____

10. _____

If you don't already have a database of customers, it's time to build one. You'll want to promote your product or service to everyone you know, regardless of whether you think they can use your product or service. People know people, and they will spread the word when properly trained how to do so.

Another quick and easy way to increase your database is just to simply go out and meet people! Go to coffee shops, functions, dinners . . . anywhere there are potential customers. If you meet just 2 people a day, your database will grow by 730 people a year. Those folks are all either potential customers or referral sources for your ideal clients.

3. INCREASE YOUR AVERAGE TRANSACTION SIZE

When I first got into real estate, my mentor Jack McDonald told me something that was so simple I overlooked it for years. He said, "Knolly, the bigger the price tag on the house, the bigger your paycheck, and you don't have to work any harder for the big paychecks." Of course, I did the opposite of what he said for years. I went after the low-hanging fruit because of my limited beliefs and lack of confidence. I went to work listing homes valued between $100,000 and $200,000 when I could have just as easily been listing homes between $1,000,000 and $2,000,000 and earned 10 times more on every sale.

Many entrepreneurs make the mistake of getting pigeonholed into a low price point or low transaction size and they stay there for far too long. It can definitely be a great place to cut your teeth and gain confidence, but once you've learned the ropes, it's time to set higher standards. If you are in sales, why not begin going after larger accounts, the ones that can order 10 times the amount of your average current accounts? If you own a service business, why not go after affluent clientele who can pay more or purchase much bigger packages?

Glenn Sanford founded a small real estate company called eXp Realty in 2009. It has since become the fastest-growing real estate brokerage in world history. How? Well, Sanford has an interesting strategy when it comes to setting goals. He begins with a goal and then quadruples it. For example, let's say you want to earn $250,000 in income this year. Quadruple your goal and go for $1 million. This will cause you to evaluate all of your strategies and business plans, and elevate them to a new level, because the strategy you would have implemented to earn $250,000 could be a very different strategy from one designed to generate $1 million or more.

Think of 5 to 10 ways you can begin increasing the average transaction size of each order or sale you make and write them below:

1. _____

2. _____

3. _____

4. _____

5. _____

6. _____

7. _____

8. _____

9. _____

10. _____

4. INCREASE THE NUMBER OF TRANSACTIONS PER CUSTOMER OR PER SALESPERSON

Another handy idea to quadruple your sales is to think of ways that you can increase the number of transactions you have with each of your existing customers. You may have to get creative with this.

Let me give you an example of what I'm doing in one of my businesses. I currently own Mentorship Masters (powered by eXp Realty). On each sale, the commission earned is split: 80 percent to my agent and 20 percent to eXp. One of the primary ways I increase the number of transactions that I get paid on is by offering my agents tons of free training on how to generate more leads. The more business they generate, the more income they produce. And the more money they make, the more I make. It's a win-win.

Then, through my partnership with eXp, I'm able to take it to a whole new level. eXp incentivizes our agents to increase their number of transactions with huge rewards. For example, once they hit a relatively easy performance goal, eXp returns 100 percent of the commission split they paid to the company during the previous 12 months (in the form of a company stock award). This further incentives my agents to hit that benchmark and produce more. Another win-win.

If you don't have a sales team, you can increase the number of transactions per customer by offering incentives directly to the customer, creating an autoship program, creating a monthly membership program, quantity discounts, and/or myriad other ways.

Below, list 5 to 10 ways to increase the number of transactions you have with your customers and clients:

1. _____

2. _____

3. _____

4. _____

5. _____

6. _____

7. _____

8. _____

9. _____

10. _____

5. RAISE YOUR PRICES

Another key strategy that can help you quadruple your income is to increase your prices. When you charge higher prices, you can provide far better service, because you can finance those upgraded services with the additional revenues that you've created. Not only that, but you get to work with a much higher level of clientele. Your customer avatar upgrades to those who can afford your rates. Increasing your prices forces you to provide services that are commensurate with the rates you are charging and places you at another level of demand.

What I have found with the entrepreneurs that I coach and consult one-on-one is that one of the reasons they had been charging lower prices is to reach a broader number of potential clients who can afford their services. But when you do that, it puts you in the same boat as everyone else and it does not differentiate you or your product from the rest. When you begin offering a premium or luxury service, you can charge quite a bit more and work with fewer clients and prospects in order to generate the revenue you desire.

Imagine for a moment that one of your affluent clients or customers is having heart trouble and is in need of a very delicate surgery. Do you suppose that they will shop for the cheapest surgeon on the market or try to compare rates? Not at all. Chances are they will gladly pay whatever it takes (within reason) to get the best surgeon they can find to perform the surgery. Likewise, you are providing a very important service or product for someone's business or lifestyle, and they should desire to have it, whatever the cost. If this is not the case, do what is necessary to increase the perceived value of your products and services. Maybe it's time for a rebrand. This idea is so important that I recently finished a 10-week training series, *Creating Your Million Dollar Value Proposition*, with my Knolly Coaching Club. Yes, I spent 10 weeks helping them build this foundation, because it is that important. You can access this free training by joining my Knolly Coaching Club at KnollyCoaching.com. (This coaching club was $297/month, but I have sponsored the cost, so there is no cost to you to join.)

The chief reason that you aren't entering into the luxury or affluent marketplace right now is fear. Maybe deep down you don't feel worthy of working with affluent clients so you lower your standards down to your comfort level. Most entrepreneurs and business leaders are just downright afraid to work with those who make a lot of money. They fear that they will come off as fakes or imposters. Sometimes they believe these folks will be more difficult to work with. I can tell you from experience that working with wealthy clients beats working with those who are broke, hands down. Those who are always looking for discount services are not your ideal clients. Of course, you can still serve that market by providing free training on your YouTube channel.

As we have already discussed, you get paid in direct proportion to the perceived value that you bring to the marketplace. When you increase your perceived value, people will flock to you and gladly pay you more money. Stop being a commodity and begin being the uniquely gifted entrepreneur that you are.

Below, make a core list of your current products/services and list how you can raise your prices. Also, think of any services that you could add to your repertoire that would allow you to charge a lot more for your services:

1. _____

2. _____

3. _____

4. _____

5. _____

6. _____

7. _____

8. _____

9. _____

10. _____

FROM $0 TO $100,000 FAST

These five strategies work whether you are new to your business or have been in business for decades. One of my many success stories is Mina Slaughter, a real estate agent from San Antonio, Texas. Some years ago, she was working as a showing assistant; I had her show some houses to a client of mine. She was charging me $25 per house. As I got to know her, I realized that she had a lot more potential than the job she was doing. I let her know that she was intelligent and could make a lot more money if she would focus her real estate practice on listings. She confided that she was struggling in real estate and that she had not made any money in eight months! Her husband insisted that if she was unable to bring in any money within 90 days, she was going to have to go back to her corporate job, which she hated. She told me that I was her last and final hope. If what I told her to do *did not* work, she would have to give up her dream of being an entrepreneur. I invited Mina to partner with me, and, I assured her, if she did what I told her to do, she would be making good money within just a few months. I also jokingly told her that within a few years of coaching with me, her husband would be asking *her* for a job.

I knew in my heart that Mina could make more than $250,000 a year and have an amazing work schedule. I started teaching Mina some high-level principles and gave her some book assignments. Her belief before was that being successful was hard; at the very least, she could not see a way to success. She had also bought into the belief that the road to succeed was painful and arduous. I had to get her to believe otherwise. Then, we went to work.

You already know that the reason most entrepreneurs don't succeed is due to their mindset. Their limiting beliefs are causing a block in their subconscious mind, which is preventing their ultimate success, since 95 percent of our daily activities are autonomic, taking place in our subconscious.*† The first thing I

---

* Gail Marra, "9 interesting facts about your subconscious mind," Gail Marra Clinical Hypnotherapy, November 11, 2021, https://www .gailmarrahypnotherapy.com/9-interesting-facts-about-your-subconscious -mind/#:~:text=The%20Subconscious%20Mind%20controls%2095%20percent %20of%20your%20life&text=Todays%20science%20estimates%20that%2095 ,that%20lies%20beyond%20conscious%20awareness.
† Bill and Rich Sones, "Strange but true: 95 percent of brain activity is unconscious," *The Oklahoman*, October 9, 2018, https://www.oklahoman.com /story/lifestyle/2018/10/09/strange-but-true-95-percent-of-brain-activity-is -unconscious/60496296007/.

taught Mina was how to rewire the way she thinks so she was only attracting things that were beneficial to her success. The truth is, what you desire desires you.

While there are very specific activities you have to do with the right mindset, I learned from my teachers that to achieve success, you have to do the right things in the right order. Mina began by creating a timebox, doing lead generation every day from 9 to 11 a.m. (Creating a timebox is the process of carving out a specific block of time to focus on specific activities.) I taught her all of my techniques and how to do them based on her personality profile. She is more of an introvert, so I taught her to pick a real estate niche based on her profile. She began acting in her zone of genius and went to work.

Soon, she gained momentum. She was doing the work and she got her very first appointment with a stranger (a prospect who was not in her SOI). Before she went on the appointment, I taught her the process of converting fear into excitement. Fear and excitement have the very same physical and internal manifestations; so, if you know how, you can channel the energy of fear and transform it into excitement. She went on the listing appointment and absolutely CRUSHED IT. She got her first listing and quickly put a cool $13,000 into her bank account.

After that experience, Mina knew in her heart that she would never again have a problem with meeting prospective clients and getting them to trust her with the sale of their most valuable asset: their home. She also would never again doubt herself. You couldn't stop her. After her first 90 days with my organization, she generated more income than she had the previous year.

Because she is a rock star, Mina quickly got overwhelmed with a ton of business and needed leverage to grow. Once again, she applied my 3 Hours a Day system to solve that problem.

She filled in the gaps and delegated the tasks she considered her weak points to others. Mina has created a phenomenal lifestyle. Recently, she reported that in the next 30 days, she will be closing on $1,800,000 in production, which will put $54,000 in her bank account. Pretty cool considering she had not made that much money in her first full year in real estate—and this is only her third year as an entrepreneur. I expect she will easily make $400,000 this year if she keeps following the 3 Hours a Day path, and I'm sure she will because it's addictive! Oh, and her husband, John, completed his real estate classes and joined her team, just like I predicted! Mina's income allowed him to retire from his job at the university.

Mina's story shows that you can and will succeed if you follow the seven steps of 3 Hours a Day exactly as they are laid out.

NEXT STEPS

Now that you've taken an insightful look at how to quadruple your income, decide on which of the five strategies discussed in this chapter you are going to implement. Of course, you should definitely implement strategy number one (delegate your business), since you are following 3 Hours a Day. However, any of the additional four are completely up to you. You can implement all or just a few of these and your income is sure to soar. There will be challenges along the way, but in the next chapter I am going to show you how to overcome them.

CHAPTER 10

Overcoming the Challenges of 3 Hours a Day

By following 3 Hours a Day, you have chosen to live your life radically different from most of your peers. You've already tried the hustle and grind and you can clearly see where that leads long-term. Now you are trying a fresh approach. Never again will you miss your child's soccer game or ballet practice, your family reunion or a night out with your favorite friends. You can finally plan that Alaskan cruise you've been putting off. You can live your life in balance and have time for all of the things in life that are near and dear to you.

But with all of the benefits that are garnered by following 3 Hours a Day, there are still some challenges that will need to be met head-on and overcome.

THE STIGMA OF LAZINESS

One of the primary challenges with 3 Hours a Day is the stigma of laziness: Won't my friends think I'm lazy if I'm not working all the time? Sadly, entrepreneurs have been brainwashed into believing that hard work alone produces the best results. I'll be the first to admit that hard work is definitely a requirement during the start-up phase, but in the long run, I have found that working smarter is what will allow you to scale quickly and crush your goals. Even when we can see that this is not the truth, it is difficult to psychologically get on board with doing things in a new way, especially when you are used to doing them per the status quo.*

I got married at the age of 22. About six months after our wedding day, Josie's mom came to visit; she never left. She was 70 years old when she first came to stay with us in a small home we were renting in South Austin. She loved it. Josie and I doted on her as if she were a queen (and she truly was); we had a most remarkable life with her. She passed away at the age of 93. During the final 10 years of her life, she battled with Alzheimer's disease. It was tough.

Josie had previously made a commitment to take care of her mother as long as she was physically and financially able to do so, and that we would keep her at the house and provide for her care. Eventually, the disease took such a toll that round-the-clock care was needed, and we initially hired two attendants. Soon, Josie had a team of seven employees. I would jokingly comment that Josie's staff was bigger than mine, and I owned three companies.

As the caregivers came to the house, I would go about my usual day, working a few hours in the morning and then spending the rest of the day as I desired. Finally, one of her workers couldn't contain the question any longer; they just simply had to know: "Why doesn't your husband work?"

---

* https://www.cnbc.com/2019/03/20/stanford-study-longer-hours-doesnt-make -you-more-productive-heres-how-to-get-more-done-by-doing-less.html

Josie was confused at first by the question. "What do you mean?" she retorted. "He does work. He works from home."

"Yes, but we hardly ever see him doing any work."

It never occurred to Josie and me how our lifestyle might appear from the outside looking in, but her worker made a valid point. Since Josie's mom spoke only Spanish, all of the workers were Spanish-speaking, and in their Latino culture, a man who sits around the house all day and doesn't go out and work (hustle) is not very highly regarded. Even when Josie explained to them that I actually do work a few hours a day and that I owned several businesses, it just didn't add up. How could a guy who hangs around the house most of the time be anything but lazy? Either that, or maybe he's secretly a drug dealer.

It will be difficult for most people in society to understand your lifestyle and how you can be earning $250,000, $500,000, or more than $1,000,000 per year while working just three hours a day. You may also be going on four or five nice vacations a year, taking nights and weekends off, and be debt-free. To the onlooker, that's simply an impossibility unless you are doing something illegal.

Because working a 12-hour day can produce monetary results in the short term, it may be difficult at first for you to clearly see that only about 10 to 15 percent of the activities that you are doing during your hustle and grind are resulting in 85 to 90 percent of the results. 3 Hours a Day is about working in a fresh new way. You are trading the busywork for smart work, and living life by design as a result.

It is obvious that there are a lot of activities that must happen in your business in order for it to stay productive and thriving, it just isn't necessary for *you* to do most of those activities. That's the power of 3 Hours a Day. Don't pay heed to the naysayers. Instead, measure the results that you get when you put 3 Hours a Day to work in your business.

WHEN THE GAME KEEPS
CALLING YOUR NAME

Another huge challenge to overcome is the desire to get back in the game. The hustle and grind is a narcotic, and it will always be calling you back onto the dance floor. You'll want to constantly remind yourself where you belong.

When I first began teaching 3 Hours a Day, I was stepping out of full-time production to fully focus on coaching and training. In the real estate game, I was a beast, selling more than 1,000 homes during my first 10 years in the business. I made tons of money and the work came easily to me, and I was working less than 3 Hours a Day. Yet for me, I felt it was time to pay it forward and share the secrets of my success.

When I stepped out of real estate production, I set a daily reminder on my phone that reads:

> *You will oftentimes desire to get back into full-time real estate production. This desire will stem from the "thrill of the game" and the resulting high income. You must shake off such urges. Your life is about focusing on your purpose and there is no room for selfishness there.*

This notification helped me in those moments when the hustle and grind was calling me back. It's a reminder to not ever fall off the 3 Hours a Day bandwagon. This lifestyle is just too amazing to fall back into the old paradigm. I encourage you to create for yourself a weekly or daily reminder as well. You can also type it up and place it in a prominent place where you will see it often.

I GOT THIS! FULL SPEED AHEAD!

Another big challenge to 3 Hours a Day is attempting to go it alone. I've witnessed far too many entrepreneurs grab the core principles of 3 Hours a Day and then attempt to go full speed ahead without hiring the right people or learning the right methods and end up overwhelmed. To achieve success fully, you must follow the seven steps exactly as they are laid out in this book. I have also given you a visual of this on the 3 Hours a Day blueprint in the Introduction. You can download a free mini poster of it by going to 3HoursADay.com/bookresources. If you feel like you need another big boost, I invite you to attend my 3 Hours a Day virtual boot camp by going to KnollyBootcamp.com.

When you first picked up a Rubik's Cube, no doubt it looked so easy! You just have to move all of the same colors to each side. Sure, it's easy enough in concept, but only a precise system will yield success each and every time. Don't get hung up on the mistake I've seen others stumble over: once they feel that they get the gist of 3 Hours a Day, they begin cutting their hours and working less without first putting all their systems in place. I'm set, they say to themselves.

When you pull the trigger prematurely, you get overwhelmed with business and don't have the bandwidth to handle everything because you don't yet have the right leverage in place. You will then find that your sales or service can begin to slip. If you don't follow the critical steps in the 3 Hours a Day system, you could end up worse than where you started. Having your business rise only to implode is a tragedy that you can easily avoid by following the steps in order as prescribed.

Resist the temptation to deviate from the plan. One missed step can have you spiraling in the wrong direction. My system is easy to follow—and it *must be followed in order.* Remember that

145

success is about doing the right things in the right order. Don't try to reinvent the wheel.

WHAT AM I GOING TO DO WITH ALL MY FREE TIME?

A neighbor of mine was recently describing the life of one of our fellow neighbors. He is single, in his seventies, and he lives to work. He comes home exhausted and spends any free time he has working around the house and recuperating from work. But it seems like he doesn't know any other way. If his work were suddenly stripped from him, what would he do?

It's ironic that one of the challenges for my students who have adopted 3 Hours a Day has been not knowing what to do with all their free time. Some of them went from working 10 hours per day to 3 hours a day in less than six months. This, in effect has opened up a big gaping hole of time in their daily calendar and they just don't know what to do with it. It's a good problem to have.

If you find yourself in this boat, the reason why you are running into a challenge with having so much free time is because you have never truly learned how to live. You can now begin living, perhaps for the first time. I am so happy for you. It is time to begin exploring all of the areas on the Life Abundance Wheel that you learned about in Chapter 4. Yes, it will be scary at first. You may even have times when you feel guilty for not working. Seeing others working their life away while you are enjoying the afternoon on the beach or touring Europe will be weird for a while. False guilt and shame can set in and attempt to rob you of your newfound freedom. Don't let it! You are now experiencing life the way it is meant to be lived.

THE BLOWBACK OF
WORKING SO HARD

One of the top regrets of those on their deathbed is wishing they hadn't worked so hard. While there are some challenges that come with 3 Hours a Day, there are myriad more challenges that come with working 8 to 12 hours each day. Just like the guy who eats nothing but junk food, there is a blowback. The blowback I'm talking about is to your health.

Stress levels around the world are at an all-time high. Poor lifestyle choices and an incessant workload can eventually take a huge toll on your adrenal glands, your brain, your heart, your kidneys, and other major organs. Health problems of all kinds can begin to set in at the cellular level and rob you of the full life you deserve to live.

3 Hours a Day allows you to live a more balanced life, so that you can be healthier overall. You can now begin to focus on all 14 life areas, as discussed in Chapter 4.

GUILT, FEAR, AND SHAME

It is an evolutionary feature of the human brain to keep you safe. One of its primary strategies to do so is to keep you focused on the familiar. To do this, it governs you using a combination of fear, guilt, and shame.

Inevitably, when you strike out to do anything new you will get hit with a chemical cocktail that will trigger one or more of these emotions. Thoughts like What do you mean you're only going to work three hours a day—are you lazy or what? or You're not cut out for a relaxed lifestyle! May creep up as you transition over to 3 Hours a Day. The root of these feelings is oftentimes fear. But the very fact that you are a business leader and entrepreneur shows that you have developed a way to rise above your emotions and do the thing that you have set your heart on. When adopting 3 Hours a Day you will need to lean into this ability all the more, because your mind will be in panic mode.

To squash these feelings, you don't want to try and simply ignore them. Instead, acknowledge them. Experience each feeling and feel it fully, acknowledging that it is there. You can also seek to understand a little bit about *why* the feeling is there, but realize that knowing the why behind the feeling is not necessary. The feeling is there because the subconscious mind wants to keep you safe. Simply acknowledge the feeling, allow it to be there, feel it fully, and let it go.

The "What If" Technique

One helpful technique I use to better understand the origin of my feelings is asking myself three questions: "what for?," "why?," and "what if?" This technique helps you get to the bottom or the root of an emotion, so that you can then face it.

Example:

I love the idea of 3 Hours a Day in concept but I feel like I should be working 8 to 10 hours a day.

What for?

Well, because that's what I've always done and that's what my parents have always done.

Why?

Because they had bills to pay and needed money!

Why?

Because if they didn't have money they would lose everything they had worked for.

And what if that did happen?

Well, they would then be on the street and they wouldn't be able to take care of us kids.

And what if that happened?

Well, then we would have been placed in a foster home and separated from each other.

And what if that happened?

We would be raised by strangers and we could have had a terrible childhood.

And so on and so forth. You will find that when you play these worst-case scenarios out they typically end in loss, and they almost always, when fully played out, end in death. Fear of loss is the great fear of the subconscious mind and it will seek to protect you from that at all costs.

When you review these scenarios that your brain has concocted, you will typically see that most of the storylines your mind has concocted are really quite bizarre and comical. Allow yourself to look at them with a bit of humor. In most cases, you will also see that there are ways for you to easily rectify or repair the situation, should your worst case scenario truly occur.

Review your worst-case scenario and ask yourself these three questions: (1) What is a more probable or positive outcome? (2) What is my inaction costing me financially, emotionally, and physically? (3) What is a more appropriate course of action for me to take so that I can achieve the results I desire?

3 Hours a Day is about gaining, not losing. You gain more time, more money, and the ability to work from anywhere in the world. You gain back your freedom of choice, which had been greatly handicapped due to your work schedule. You also gain health, vitality, and peace of mind. You gain a plethora of the things you have been neglecting in the 14 life areas.

A LIFE OF NO REGRETS

Not only does 3 Hours a Day empower you to live the life of your dreams, it also allows you to live a life with no regrets. Once I was no longer trying to prove myself to others, I found a big sense of purpose. One big wake-up call for me was when I heard about Bronnie Ware's *Top Five Regrets of the Dying*. Bronnie Ware was an Australian palliative care nurse who spent several years exclusively caring for patients in their final 12 weeks of life. She noted that "the regrets touch upon being more genuine, not working so hard, expressing one's true feelings, staying in touch with friends and finding more joy in life."*

Think about your own life. What might you regret if you kept on the path you've been on? What is your legacy going to be? As morbid as it may sound, I want you to take a look at your end and start working backward. Think about what kind of life

---

* Bronnie Ware, *The Top Five Regrets of the Dying: A Life Transformed by the Dearly Departing* (Carlsbad: Hay House, Inc., 2012).

will ensure that you feel fulfilled, happy, and have zero regrets upon your ultimate exit. Imagine the kind of life you want to live and start to live your life by design. Become the master of your destiny. Begin to fully adopt 3 Hours a Day, and you too will have everything in this life that you've ever wanted.

CHAPTER 11

Frequently Asked Questions About 3 Hours a Day

Once again, congratulations are in order! You have made it through the book and have committed to begin your journey to 3 Hours a Day. As you continue to implement this system, I have no doubt that you will see marvelous upgrades in both your business and your personal life.

In this chapter, I am going to review some of the most frequently asked questions that I get about 3 Hours a Day to help you better understand it and to help you implement it at a deeper level. You will want to reference this chapter often if you have any issues or questions that arise during your journey.

What is 3 Hours a Day?

3 Hours a Day is a system developed by Knolly Williams (the Business Healer), which allows business leaders and entrepreneurs to quadruple their income while working just three hours a day.

How does 3 Hours a Day work?

3 Hours a Day is a seven-step process that teaches you to systematize, automate, and delegate your business so that you can unlock the holy grail of freedom: time freedom, location freedom, and financial freedom. During your 3 Hours a Day you will focus on two Big Picture Priorities and everything else will be delegated to someone else.

Can I begin implementing 3 Hours a Day immediately?

Yes! You can begin implementing 3 Hours a Day in your business by starting with Step 1 today. There is no need to wait. I do not recommend you scale back your work hours initially. That will come in due time, as you fully implement my system.

Does implementing 3 Hours a Day mean I will cut my workday down to three hours a day?

Yes, eventually you will be working just three hours a day—or less in some cases. Initially, however, you will begin by implementing 3 Hours a Day within your current work schedule.

When starting out with 3 Hours a Day, you will begin by creating a timebox, where you only focus on your two Big Picture Priorities for three hours each day. At first, you will still be doing many of the tasks you do now outside of your timebox. Once you begin to implement Step 4 (delegate your business), you can start to cut down your workday. I cover this in more detail in Chapter 6. For example, I currently work about three hours per week in my real estate business and my real estate group still sells hundreds of homes a year.

I have found that many entrepreneurs love to work, so reducing your work schedule to less than three hours per day may not be appealing to most. On the other hand, if you are not deeply fulfilled in your business even when focusing on your unique superpower, you can delegate everything in your operation and just oversee it, spending just a few hours a week doing so.

How soon will it be before I can cut my daily work hours down to three hours per day?

How quickly you can dwindle your workday down to three hours per day depends on where your current business is now and how quickly you can adopt the steps of 3 Hours a Day. If you already have leverage in your business that you can quickly assign once you graduate to Step 4, then it may be possible for you to implement 3 Hours a Day within a few weeks or months. Others may take nine months to a year—or two—to fully integrate all seven steps into their business.

Ultimately, how long it takes doesn't really matter. You now have a goal in mind and instead of simply jumping on the treadmill every day with no end in sight, you now have a blueprint and a game plan to get to 3 Hours a Day. Most entrepreneurs work for 20, 30, or 40 years without ever being able to cut their work hours significantly. Even if it takes you two years to fully implement 3 Hours a Day, you will be ahead of 99 percent of entrepreneurs on the planet.

Give yourself the time and the grace to do it right the first time. Follow each of my steps exactly and don't try to rush success. Trying to speed up the process typically ends in disaster (or, at least, less than optimal results). Remember that SLOW is the fastest way to get rich. Take your time.

I am experiencing some psychological challenges with implementing 3 Hours a Day. I'm beginning to doubt myself.

Experiencing psychological and emotional challenges when implementing 3 Hours a Day is quite normal. This just means that your subconscious mind has kicked in and it is trying to put the brakes on. It doesn't like change and wants to keep things status quo. You already know in your heart that 3 Hours a Day is what you desire, so keep moving forward by transcending your feelings. Realize that your thoughts and your feelings are *part of you* but they are not *YOU*. Oftentimes, our mental body and our emotional body are acting out of fear, especially fear of change or the unknown.

Go back and read Chapter 10, where I expound further on the challenges of 3 Hours a Day and how to overcome them. I also provide tons of tips, tricks, and techniques to help you further your journey on my weekly podcast and on my YouTube channel. If you feel you need my personal mentoring and coaching to help keep you on track, join my free Knolly Coaching Club at KnollyCoaching.com.

Can 3 Hours a Day be adopted by any business?

Yes, it is possible to adopt 3 Hours a Day to any business, even one where you are trading time for dollars. Some years ago, I shared my system with Juliann, my massage therapist. When I first began coaching her, she did everything in her business herself. She did the marketing, booked the clients, and rendered services. If she wasn't physically present and performing her job, she didn't get paid. Using my 3 Hours a Day system, Juliann was able to go from running her massage business all by herself to having a thriving practice with multiple locations. She went from being a one-woman show to hiring a team of more than 40 licensed massage therapists to perform various services. She oversees the entire operation and gets a healthy percentage of the revenue from every service rendered.

Less than a year after implementing 3 Hours a Day, Juliann broke her foot and couldn't work for months. Because she had already implemented my system into her business, she was able to recuperate at home without skipping a beat in her income. She told me frankly, "Knolly, if it hadn't been for you, I would have lost my house."

I own multiple businesses. Can I still adopt 3 Hours a Day?

Yes! I personally own three businesses and I work just three hours per day. Don't get the idea that you have to work three hours a day per business. Not at all. Many of my coaching clients own multiple companies and have successfully adopted 3 Hours a Day.

To do this successfully, you will want to have no more than one point of contact for each business. That means no more than one employee or VA that reports directly to you. You will create a chain of command where all of your other team members will be somewhere underneath that individual. In my companies,

3 HOURS A DAY

I have an operations manager who oversees the business. All other team members are under that individual.

I'm experiencing trouble hiring the right people. How do I go about hiring the right team?

When it comes to hiring your team, this has to be done right the first time or your will experience setbacks in your business. Go back and study Chapter 6 in detail and follow the steps exactly as laid out.

I'm having a hard time adopting the concept of 3 Hours a Day. My clients love me and they won't work with anyone else! What can I do?

No matter how amazing you are, you have to realize that you *are* replaceable.

I remember when I was 38 years old and selling tons of real estate in Austin. I genuinely believed that no one in town was better than me. Out of 9,800 real estate agents in the city, my production as a solo agent was ranked number one by the *Austin Business Journal*, even further solidifying the fact that I was the cat's meow. But I was also running myself into the ground.

One day I had an epiphany and realized that if I were to drop dead, it would be maybe three or four years before most of my clients forgot my name. Within five years, most of my colleagues and competitors would have forgotten my name as well. I was working way too hard for far too little. After that epiphany, I hired Susan to begin going on all of my appointments. I trained her in my system and she did a marvelous job. She replaced me in the field and my clients loved her. The real truth is, your clients will love doing business with the folks you bring onto your team, provided you hire right.

I'm ready to retire and leave the business altogether. What's my next step?

In truth, 3 Hours a Day is semiretirement as it is, although I prefer to think of it more as a way of life. If you are ready to completely walk away from your business, though, your options might be to sell it outright, sell and retain an ownership interest, or simply hire a business partner to completely take over your business.

Another option is to cut your workweek down to between three and five hours. To do this, you will want to follow all of the steps of 3 Hours a Day exactly as laid out. The only deviation you will make is that you will also be hiring a business partner who can do your two Big Picture Priorities, in effect replacing yourself. Instead of hiring the opposite of you, that person might need to be a match for your zone of genius and possess your same or similar superpower. This way you can hand over the reins and spend between just three and five hours a week overseeing the operation. Do not do this alone. Be sure to hire a coach to guide you through this process.

I've been following 3 Hours a Day and I just can't seem to stay on track. Invariably, I slip back into a longer workday. What should I do?

Your problem is psychological. We've all heard stories of prisoners who obtain their freedom only to find that living a life without someone else telling them what to do every hour of the day proves too much for them. Invariably, they sabotage their own success and fabricate a scheme that causes them to become incarcerated once again. Your brain and subconscious will do anything to keep you safe. Whenever you are going into unfamiliar and uncharted territory the subconscious will do whatever it takes to get you back to where you were.

A good idea is to look at exactly where you are falling off track. Retrace the seven steps on my 3 Hours a Day blueprint to find out exactly which step you are tripping up on. Again, this is all psychological work, and there may be an unconscious block that is preventing you from having the success that you desire. Use the *what for* technique that I talked about in the previous chapter to get to the bottom of what is holding you back.

Identifying the problem puts you 90 percent closer to the solution. Oftentimes, private coaching sessions, clearing sessions, or business healing sessions are required in order for you to fully move forward in victory. I do offer private one-on-one consultation sessions if you need my personal help. Go to Knolly .com for more info.

3 Hours a Day makes so much sense! Why doesn't every business adopt this system?

Many things that make perfect sense are not easily adopted by most. 3 Hours a Day is a radical system and involves change. Change is the least favorite thing for the subconscious mind to do. Therefore, most will defy logic and reason in order to maintain the status quo. Or, even more sinisterly, the *inner you* will completely sabotage your efforts. As the saying goes, "Sometimes the enemy is the *inner me*."

If systems that made the most sense were routinely adopted, schools, governments, and cities would be run quite differently. Don't focus on what others are doing or not doing. Focus on the success that you desire and utilize 3 Hours a Day to help you realize your wildest dreams.

Help! I know that 3 Hours a Day is the system I need but I can't seem to fully get on board. How can I build my belief in the system so that I can begin seeing the results in my life and business?

One of the big things that I try to do with 3 Hours a Day is help build your belief, because without belief you cannot achieve ultimate success. Take a look at all of the students who are achieving success by following 3 Hours a Day. Hardly a week goes by where I don't introduce another person on my podcast or YouTube channel who is having massive success with my system. To help build your belief, check out 3HoursADay.com to review case studies of others who are succeeding.

As I previously explained, when presented with anything radical and new, your subconscious will try to shut it down by introducing doubt, fear, guilt, and shame. Eventually though, as you begin experiencing the most profound success of your life through the adaptation of 3 Hours a Day, you will actually move beyond belief. In other words you will no longer need to *believe* in this system.

For me, I don't merely believe in 3 Hours a Day. I KNOW that it is a life-changing system, providing true transformation for all who are brave enough to fully adopt it. I have seen the results daily in my own business and time and time again in the lives and businesses of my students.

I'm having trouble trying to figure out exactly what I should be doing during my 3 Hours a Day.

What you should be doing during your 3 Hours a Day will be determined by two things: (1) your unique superpower, and (2) where you are in your business.

I discussed this in greater detail in Chapter 8. If your business is bringing in more leads than you can handle, then your top problem will be not having enough time. Your solution to this problem is leverage. If your business is not bringing in enough leads, then your problem will be money. You solve this problem by bringing in more leads (cash flow) and increasing your lead conversion skills.

During your 3 Hours a Day, you will be focusing on two Big Picture Priorities. If you have a money problem, your two Big Picture Priorities will probably be lead generation and sales. If you have a time problem, your two Big Picture Priorities will likely be branding and leadership. While the two Big Picture Priorities I mentioned above are going to typically be the biggest boulders that need to be moved in your business, exactly what you personally decide to focus on during your 3 Hours a Day will be further be determined by your superpower. Go back to Chapters 3 and 8 to study this further.

At the start of each workday, there should be no question as to what exactly you should be doing to most effectively move the needle in your business. If you are still confused, be sure to hire a coach and join my free coaching club.

Does 3 Hours a Day work for retirees?

3 Hours a Day is a highly beneficial philosophy and strategy for entrepreneurs, however the principles work even if you are retired!

Retirees certainly won't get the maximum benefit out of this book, but if you are retired, you will surely benefit from incorporating the core concepts contained herein. By adopting 3 Hours a Day into your retired life, you will have blueprints for time management and how to complete everything you would like to do during your precious golden years.

I've been following 3 Hours a Day for about a year and I love it! It has been absolutely life-changing. I'm now in the process of a merger and I'm finding that I am working more like I used to. Recently, I worked seven hours! Am I going backward?

You will find that, from time to time, you will need to adjust your schedule, especially when you are taking on a new project like an acquisition, a merger, the launch of a new product, a new partnership, launching a new podcast or TV show, etc. As you take on these new projects, you may need to adjust your schedule to work more, and that's OK.

The beauty of 3 Hours a Day is that it serves as an anchor, bringing your business back into homeostasis when the time comes, and it keeps you focused on the two Big Picture Priorities. You can and you will get back to 3 Hours a Day, but for now allow yourself the grace to work the additional time necessary to launch your new project. In fact, you will still work your 3 Hours a Day and simply add on the additional hours you need for your new project. If it takes three months or six months or even a year of working this revised schedule, so be it. Know that it is a limited-time gig and you will be returning back to your regular schedule after a fixed period of time. It's all good. Enjoy your new project and knock the ball out of the park!

Should I hire a coach?

YES! Having coaches and mentors is essential for you to reach your ultimate greatness. Every major athlete, celebrity, and politician has a coach, and you should, too. If you want to succeed at the top level, hire the right coach. Keep in mind that coaching is not an expense; it is an investment. A good coach will help you earn at least 10 times the amount of their fee.

One of the things I did right when I first got started in the real estate business was hire a coach. I needed help badly, and I didn't want to repeat the same mistakes I had made in my former profession, so I invested thousands of dollars a month to help me fill in the gaps, get to success quicker, and help point out my blind spots.

When I first hired Coach Julie, she asked me what my goals were. I was super proud to inform her that my goal was to list and sell 40 homes a year. In truth, I would have been happy if I sold just 20 homes a year, but I doubled the number, thinking it would impress my new coach. I thought this goal would sound incredibly ambitious, given that the average seasoned agent in Austin, Texas, at the time was selling between six and eight homes a year and I had only been licensed for eight months.

Coach Julie completely burst my bubble. She asked, "Why not set a goal of 100 deals per year?" That suggestion seemed so totally crazy to me that I laughed out loud.

"I don't want to work that much," I told her. I was on track my first year to close about 40 deals and I was already pulling my hair out! Julie confidently and matter-of-factly pointed out that if I did 100 deals per year, I could work half as much as if I did 40. That made absolutely no sense to me, but I trusted my coach. What I came to understand was that if you set up the right system, it's like a factory pumping out products. Once you have the system in place, you can pump out as much product as you want. By my second year, I did over 80 deals and I never sold less than 100 deals per year after that. In fact, my last year in production I sold 153 homes and I worked about three hours per week in my real estate business. I was completely leveraged and had a team of Admins running my entire operation from A to Z.

I could not have achieved that level of success if I had chosen to stay small. Coach Julie was right. I worked way less than half as much and eventually made more than four times as much money through the gift of leverage. The big lesson that I learned is that hard work doesn't necessarily equate to a ton of money. Even when I worked really, really hard and made a lot of money as a result, the fruit of that labor just wasn't as sweet. But working three hours per day, working smarter not harder, and still making tons of money? That feels really good.

If you feel stuck and want to inquire about how I can personally coach you and help you reach your ultimate goals, you can learn more on my website at Knolly.com.

I really love 3 Hours a Day. How can I spread the message so that more of my colleagues can learn about this revolutionary model?

I love it! We definitely need more 3 Hour a Day soldiers out there. 3 Hours a Day leads to a life with no regrets. Sure, it sounds great to tell someone they should consider working less and enjoying more freedom, but until they have a map and a blueprint to achieve it, the advice is all but wasted words.

You can invest in those you care about by gifting them a copy of this book, or at least sending them a link to where they can order it. If you are a coach or trainer, make sure your clients

3 HOURS A DAY

get a copy of this book and feature it in a book club! This information needs to get out. Don't share your copy! This book will serve as your resource guide and a step-by-step instruction manual, so you'll always want to have it handy as you move forward in the journey. Mark it up! Highlight it! And above all, implement it!

CONCLUSION

Thank you so much for reading this revolutionary book. Now, with 3 Hours a Day, you have a very simple and easy-to-adopt system that will allow you to multiply your income while living more. I pray that your life and business will flourish as you begin to implement this framework into your daily practice. Rest assured that no matter your profession or trade, 3 Hours a Day has the power to grant you the freedom, liberty, and success that you were destined for.

ACKNOWLEDGEMENTS

First, I want to send a BIG thank you to God Almighty, a.k.a. the Source of all that is. Without You, I would be nothing.

I am so eternally grateful to my wife, Josefina (my Peet), for all your love and support over the years. I love you. You have been a true lighthouse and refuge for me.

Thanks are also in order for my team at 2 Market Media (Steve, Hank, Carly, Lauren, Kayla, Arestia, and crew). Thanks to my team at McGraw Hill for believing in me and this incredible book (Cheryl, Dannalie, Michele, Scott, Kirsten, and Jonathan).

Special shout out to all the real estate agents in my Mentorship Masters group at eXp Realty and my staff members! Thank you for partnering with me; let's take over the world (lol).

THANK YOU to my Knolly Coaching Club members. I look forward to us continuing to GROW together.

I owe a debt of gratitude to the entrepreneurs, business leaders, and real estate agents who have followed me over the years. Thank you for your love and support. I pray that this work will change your life as it has for so many others. It is truly time for us to reclaim our rightful place in society and become the leaders we are destined to be.

I want to thank YOU, the reader for investing in this book and sharing it with others. You are helping make your life and the lives of others infinitely better.

And since I've been a poet since the age of 13 (that's 40 years, lol), my acknowledgments wouldn't be complete without a short rhyme:

> The hustle and grind was alright for a time
> But it's a new season with a reason to shine,
> No need to bust you @ss like you used to do
> No need to get that cash while killin yo'self too
> 3 Hours a Day, yo that's all it takes
> Working all day long is the biggest mistake
> Live your life by design, that's the only way
> Work LESS and LIVE MORE with 3 Hours a Day!

RESOURCES

Also available at 3HoursADay.com/bookresources.

CHAPTER 2: Embracing 3 Hours a Day

Profile Tests:

Free DISC personality test: https://www.123test.com/disc-personality-test/

Free The Passion Test: https://www.thepassiontest.com/

Free Genius Test: https://app.geniusu.com/my-genius-test

CHAPTER 4: Step 2: Evaluate Your Business

Life Abundance Wheel:

3HoursADay.com/bookresources

CHAPTER 6: Step 4: Delegate Your Business

My sample task list:

THE
KN🔥LLY
TEAM
NEW LISTING CHECKLIST

PRE-LISTING

☐ Step 1. Generate seller prospect.

☐ Step 2. Initial phone consultation with seller questionnaire.

☐ Step 3. Send seller prospect your follow-up email.

☐ Step 4. Input the prospect into your database.

☐ Step 5. Do comparative market nalysis (CMA) and research.

☐ Step 6. Phone consultation with seller prospect and set the listing appointment.

☐ Step 7. Send seller prospect a follow-up email.

☐ Step 8. Drop off your pre-listing package.

☐ Step 9. Draw up the listing documents.

☐ Step 10. Confirm the listing appointment and request that the seller homework be filled out ahead of time.

☐ Step 11. Conduct the listing appointment and secure the listing.

LISTING SETUP

☐ Step 12. Collect property survey.

☐ Step 13. Prepare the house for sale.

☐ Step 14. Set up the property.

☐ Step 15. Order professional photography.

☐ Step 16. Write the property description.

☐ Step 17. Input the listing to MLS.

☐ Step 18. Upload docs to MLS.

☐ Step 19. Upload photos to the MLS.

☐ Step 20. Review the listing and make it active (GO LIVE!).

LISTING SERVICING

☐ Step 21. Set up the listing in your database and start the transaction.

☐ Step 22. Initiate and invite seller to the online transaction.

☐ Step 23. Set up an action plan for your listing.

☐ Step 24. Initiate marketing plan for your listing.

☐ Step 25. Set up electronic showing feedback.

☐ Step 26. Set up "weekly update" email drip campaign to seller with link to your CRM.

☐ Step 27. Make periodic price adjustments.

☐ Step 28. Receive and negotiate offers.

CONTRACT TO CLOSE

☐ Step 29. Update MLS status to *pending*.

☐ Step 30. Initiate closing action plan.

☐ Step 31. Congratulatory call and email to seller.

☐ Step 32. Send executed contract to seller.

☐ Step 33. Negotiate any post-inspection items.

☐ Step 34. Send *client information sheet* to escrow office.

☐ Step 35. Weekly contact and updates to seller.

☐ Step 36. Submit all documents to your compliance department.

☐ Step 37. Send DA and DI to escrow office.

☐ Step 38. Handle all closing details.

☐ Step 39. Review HUD-1 settlement statement with seller.

☐ Step 40. Attend closing.

POST-CLOSING

☐ Step 41. Send post-closing gifts to seller and buyer.

☐ Step 42. Send *Homeowner's Tip Guide* to buyer.

☐ Step 43. Update the transaction in your CRM.

☐ Step 44. Add buyer to your CRM.

☐ Step 45. Send seller your *Post-Closing Seller Survey* via email.

☐ Step 46. Pick up your sign and lockbox.

© Knolly Williams | www.SuccessWithListings.com

CHAPTER 9: Step 7: Quadruple Your Income with 3 Hours a Day

Creating Your Million Dollar Value Proposition MasterClass:

You get paid in direct proportion to the perceived value that you bring to the marketplace. If you increase your value, you get paid more. That's why creating what I call your "value proposition" is a critical first step in building your brand. You can get my 10-part series on exactly how to do that and it is absolutely FREE to Knolly Coaching Club members. If you aren't already a member, you can join by going to https://www.KnollyCoaching.com/.

INDEX

Accountability, as pillar of business, 74–75
Activities:
for lead generation, 111–112
as pillar of business, 65–66
Addiction to hustle, 11–12, 16
Administrative help, 84–85, 88–90, 93–96
Advanced 3 Hours a Day, 107
Adventure, evaluating your life for, 54, 57
Allied resources, 87–88
Areas of evaluation, 50–54
Ask and it is Given (Hicks and Hicks), 65
Attempting to go it alone, 145–146
Average transaction size, increasing, 131–132

Balance your business (step 3), xvii–xviii, 63–76
accountability, 74–75
activities, 65–66
eight pillars of business, 63–64
mindset, 64–65
money, 69–74
people, 66–67
systems, 67–68
tools, 68–69
training, 75–76
Bayerle, Nicholas, 51

Beginner 3 Hours a Day, 107
Belief(s):
limiting, 137–138
that you can do it all, 98–101
in 3 Hours a Day system, building, 161
Berry, Bryant, 4–5
Big Picture Priority(-ies), xi, xiii
branding, 119–120
change in, 15
choosing, 108–110
in determining what you do during work hours, 162
focus on, 13
lead generation, 110–114
leadership, 120–123
sales, 115–118
Blame, 60
Blowback of working so hard, 157
Books, reading, 65, 75, 76
Brain, 60
efficiency of, 129
rewiring your, 16, 65
safety as goal of, 147
Branding, as Big Picture Priority, 119–120
Breakthrough Advertising (Schwartz), 51
Burnout, 25
Business operating system, 97
Busyness, 66, 112–13

Calling, discovering your, 46–47
Career, evaluating your, 55, 57
Cash creation, 66
Chain of command, 157–158
Challenges:
overcoming (see Overcoming
challenges)
psychological, 156, 159–160
Change, 160
Chick-Fil-A, xviii
Coaches, 34
for accountability, 74–75
for 3 Hours a Day, 164–165
Compensation models, 96
Continuity income, 73
Cost(s):
of leverage, 18–21
of monthly overhead, 73
Creating money, 19–20
Creating Your Million Dollar Value
Proposition, 135
Customers:
concept of 3 Hours a Day for,
158–159
database of, 130
increasing number of, 129–130
increasing number of
transactions per, 132–134

Davis, Dawn, 101
Default living, x–xi
Delegate your business (step 4),
xviii–xix, 77–96
compensation models, 96
exercise for, 78–80
finding people to hire, 87–90
hiring the right people, 80–84
personality profile for new
hires, 85–86
positions to hire for, 84–87
to quadruple your income,
127–129
and virtual teams, 86–87

why good job descriptions are
critical, 90–95
Delegation, xi–xiii, 14
common belief about, 98
to free up your mind, 129
freedom brought by, 66–67
in lead lifecycle, 118
of 90 percent of your activities,
19, 77
systematizing through, 102
Delivery:
evaluating your, 52–54
as supporting role, 66
Design, discovering your, 35–39
Design your 3 Hours a Day (step
6), xx–xxi, 107–125
branding as Big Picture
Priority, 119–120
choosing Big Picture Priorities,
108–110
example of, 123–125
lead generation as Big Picture
Priority, 110–114
leadership as Big Picture
Priority, 120–123
sales as Big Picture Priority,
115–118
Desire(s):
divine, discovering your, 40–42
to get back in the game, 144
Destiny:
discovering your, 33–34
Discovering Your Divine Destiny
Workbook, 34–47
Diagnosing the problem, 49–50
DISC personality assessment, 22,
23, 85, 98
Discovering Your Divine Destiny
Workbook, 34–47
Distractions, 113

8-hour days, 15–16, 18
The E-Myth (Gerber), 82

Entrepreneurship:
author's experiences in, 1–9
excuses for not prospecting in,
112–114
in 3 Hours a Day, 9–12
Evaluate your business (step 2),
xvi–xvii, 49–61
diagnosing the problem, 49–50
five areas of evaluation, 50–54
and Life Abundance Wheel,
54–58
written goals, 58–59
and your mind at work, 59–61
Evaluating your life, 54–58
Exactly What to Say (Jones), 114
eXp Realty, 131, 133
Experience (being):
divine, discovering your, 42–45
as purpose of life, 33

Fair Labor Standards Act, 15
Family, evaluating your, 55, 57
Fear, 32
overcoming challenge of,
147–150
of working with wealthy
clients, 135
Feast-or-famine cycle, 109
Feel Free to Prosper (Jennet), 65
Finance function:
evaluating your, 52, 54
as supporting role, 66
Finances:
evaluating your, 55, 57
numbers in, 69–72
Focus, 13, 66
Ford, Henry, 15
Four-stage lead lifecycle, 116–118
Franchising, value of, xviii
Free products/services/items, 120
Free time, not knowing what to
do with, 146
Freedom, xxii, 66

Frequently asked questions,
153–166
Friel, James, 51
Friends, evaluating your, 55, 57
Full-time employees, 88
Fun, evaluating your life for, 54,
57

Gaskins, Tony, 4
Gerber, Michael, 82
Giving back:
evaluating your, 55, 57
as your legacy, 33
Goals:
accountability for, 74, 75
altering, 59
best practices for achieving, 68
in evaluating your business,
58–59
financial numbers to meet,
70–72
getting your mind on board
with, 60–61
quadrupling your, 131–132
setting, 30–33
Success, 120–121
Going it alone, 145–146
Grapetree Records, 4–8
Guilt:
false, 146
overcoming challenge of,
147–150

Habits, 113–114
Hard work:
blowback of, 157
income vs., 165
and stigma of laziness, 141–143
Hawkins, David, 65
Health and wellness:
blowback of hard work on, 147
evaluating your, 55, 57
Hicks, Esther, 65

Hicks, Jerry, 65
Hiring, 158
  first hire, 19, 102
  and "I've Had BAD
    EXPERIENCES Hiring
    People" myth, 23–24
  job descriptions, 90–95
  in order to delegate, 66–67,
    80–84
  personality profile for new
    hires, 81, 85–86
  positions to hire for, 84–87
  unsuccessful, reasons for,
    80–81, 83–84
Hone your superpower (step 1),
  xiv, xvi, 29–47
  discovering your destiny, 33–34
  *Discovering Your Divine Destiny
    Workbook*, 34–47
  discovering your superpower, 34
  setting your goals, 30–33

"I Could NEVER Work That
  Schedule" myth, 17–18
"I Like to WORK!" myth, 24–26
"I'm Not ORGANIZED" myth,
  21–23
Implementation:
  of systems, 68
  of 3 Hours a Day, 154
Incentives to customers, 133
Income:
  continuity, 73
  ideas leading to creation of, 129
  meeting goals for, 69–72
  in proportion to perceived
    value, 75
  setting goal for, 59–60
  (*See also* Quadruple your
    income [step 7])
Income-producing activities,
  65–66
Industrial revolution, 15
Intermediate 3 Hours a Day, 107

Intimacy, evaluating your life for,
  55, 57
"It's Like That" (Run-D.M.C.), 3
"I've Had BAD EXPERIENCES
  Hiring People" myth, 23–24

Jack's Chicken Shack, xviii
Jennet, Marilyn, 65
Job descriptions (JDs):
  for success in hiring, 81
  writing, 90–95
Jones, Phil M., 114
Justice League, 29

King's Brotherhood, 51
Knolly Coaching Club, 65, 73,
  76, 135, 156

Laziness, stigma of, 141–143
Lead capturing, 117
Lead conversion, 118
Lead generation:
  as Big Picture Priority, 110–114
  in four-stage lead lifecycle,
    116–117
Lead incubating, 117
Leadership, as Big Picture
  Priority, 120–123
Legacy (giving), 33
Letting Go (Hawkins), 65
Leverage:
  in branding, 119
  cost of, 18–21
  as golden secret, 66
  and "Leverage COSTS TOO
    MUCH" myth, 18–21
  in 3 Hours a Day, 13–14
"Leverage COSTS TOO
  MUCH" myth, 18–21
Life:
  evaluating your, 54–58, 146
  of no regrets, 150–151
Life Abundance Wheel, 54–58,
  146

Lifestyle:
  evaluating your, 55, 57
  others' misunderstanding of,
    143
  and use of free time, 146
Liking to work, 24–26
Living:
  by design, x–xii, 15
  with no regrets, 150–151

Marketing:
  evaluating your, 51, 53
  as income-producing, 66
  during promotional
    opportunities, 119–120
Marriage, evaluating your, 55, 57
Marston, William Moulton, 22
Maybury, Richard J., 74
McDonald, Jack, 131
Mentors, 164
Mentorship Master, 73, 76, 133
Mind:
  freeing up your, 129
  limiting beliefs in, 137–138
  mastering the, 165
  resistance to change in, 64–65
  as worst enemy or best friend,
    59–61
Mindset:
  as keystone pillar of business,
    64–65
  money, 69
  victim, 30
Mindshare:
  freeing up your, 127, 129
  lost, xi
Mission (doing), 33
The Modern Day Business Man
  (Bayerle), 51
Money:
  creating, 19–20
  not having enough, 108
  as pillar of business, 69–74
  (See also Income)

MoreSolds, 89
Murphy, Joseph, 65
MyOutdesk, 89
Myths of 3 Hours a Day, 16–26
  "I Could NEVER Work That
    Schedule," 17–18
  "I Like to WORK!," 24–26
  "I'm Not ORGANIZED,"
    21–23
  "I've Had BAD
    EXPERIENCES Hiring
    People," 23–24
  "Leverage COSTS TOO
    MUCH," 18–21
  "There's NO WAY!," 17

Numbers, 69–72

Objections, handling, 115–116
Operations:
  evaluating your, 52, 54
  inefficient, 97
  as supporting role, 66
Opportunities, lost, xi
Organizing daily tasks, 103–106
Overcoming challenges, 141–151
  attempting to go it alone,
    145–146
  and blowback of working so
    hard, 157
  desire to get back in the game,
    144
  of guilt, fear, and shame,
    147–150
  for a life of no regrets, 150–151
  not knowing what to do with
    free time, 146
  psychological challenges, 156
  stigma of laziness, 141–143

Passion:
  channeling, 25, 26
  divine, discovering your, 39–40
  finding your, 30

Paying others, how to afford,
19–20
People:
groups of, 31–33
as pillar of business, 66–67
the right people to delegate to,
80–84
People, systems, and tools
(PST):
to free up your time, 17
as leverage, 13–14, 66
and training, 84
Perceived value, 135–136
Perfectionism, 101
Performance reviews, 122
Personal development, evaluating
your, 55, 57
Personality profiles:
free tests for, 22–23
income-producing techniques
based on, 138
for new hires, 81, 85–86
understanding weaknesses
through, 98
Physical environment, evaluating
your, 54, 57
Pillars of business, 63–76
accountability, 74–75
activities, 65–66
mindset, 64–65
money, 69–74
people, 66–67
systems, 67–68
tools, 68–69
training, 75–76
*The Power of Your Subconscious
Mind* (Murphy), 65
Prices, raising, 134–136
Prioritization, 129
Problem, diagnosing the, 49–50
Productivity, lost years of, xi
Prospecting, 111–114
PST (*see* People, systems, and
tools)

Psychological challenges, 156,
159–160
Purpose:
channeling, 25
finding your, 30
of human beings, 33

Quadruple your income (step 7),
xxi, 127–139
by delegating your business,
127–129
example of, 136–139
by increasing average
transaction size, 131–132
by increasing number of
customers, 129–130
by increasing number of
transactions per customer
or salesperson, 132–134
by raising your prices, 134–136
Quarterly evaluations, 51
Quarterly goal objectives, 121

Raising your prices, 134–136
Ramsey, Daniel, 89
Reading, 65, 76
Rechanneling, 25
Regrets, 150–151
Relationships, evaluating your,
55, 57
Retirees:
hiring, 88
semiretiring, 159
3 Hours a Day work for,
162–163
Rewiring your brain, 16
Rios, Chris, 100–101
Rohn, Jim, 75
Roosevelt, Franklin, 15
Run-D.M.C., 3, 4

Sales:
as Big Picture Priority, 115–118
evaluating your, 51–53

going after larger accounts in, 131

as income-producing, 66

Sales processes, 109–110

Salespeople, increasing number of transactions per, 132–134

Sanford, Glenn, 131

Schedule, 17–18

and "I Could NEVER Work That Schedule," 17–18

prospecting in your, 113–114

Schwartz, Eugene, 51

Secret revenue streams (SRSs), 73

Self-worth, 26

Semiretiring, 159

Service businesses:

raising prices in, 134–135

transaction size in, 131

Shame:

false, 146

overcoming challenge of, 147–150

Slaughter, Mina, 136–139

Small Business Opportunities, xvii–xviii, 2–3

SOPs (standard operating procedures), xix

Spirituality, evaluating your, 55, 57–58

SRSs (secret revenue streams), 73

Standard operating procedures (SOPs), xix

Staying on track, 159–160

Stigma of laziness, 141–143

Strengths, 99–101

Subconscious mind, 59–61, 137–138, 160

Success:

fully achieving, 145

measuring, xi

in response to trauma, 7

sabotaging your, 60, 160

using Team Operations Bible for, 123

Success Goals, 120–121

Superpower:

in determining what you do during work hours, 162

discovering your, 29–30, 34

Discovering Your Divine Destiny Workbook, 34–47

(*See also* Hone your superpower [step 1])

Systematize your business (step 5), xix–xx, 97–106

and "I'm Not ORGANIZED" myth, 21–23

organizing daily tasks, 103–106

through delegation, 102

and trap of thinking you can do it all, 98–101

and waiting for perfection, 101

Systems:

business operating system, 97

as pillar of business, 67–68

Team Operations Bible (TOB), xix

to achieve success, 123

creating, 102–106

in hiring the right people, 81, 82

purpose of, 91

"There's NO WAY!" myth, 17

Thinking you can do it all, 98–101

"Three lead buckets," 111–112

3 Hours a Day, ix–x, 13–27

advantage of, 9–12

Big Picture Priorities in, 13

building your belief in, 161

customers' concept of, 158–159

defined, 153

difficulties in adopting, 160–161

as focus, 13

following the steps of, 145–146

3 Hours a Day (*continued*)
frequently asked questions
about, 153–166
fundamentals of, 14–15
implementing, 154–156
levels of, 107
leverage in, 13–14
and living by design vs. by
default, x–xii
making the change to, 14
myths of, 16–26
new projects requiring
adjustment in, 163
overcoming challenges in (*see*
Overcoming challenges)
psychological challenges of,
156, 159–160
reason for adopting, xii–xiv
and reasons for 8-hour days,
15–16
for retirees, 162–163
as semiretirement, 159
seven-step process for, xiv–xxi,
154 (*See also individual
steps*)
spreading the message about,
165–166
staying on track with, 159–160
time needed to cut down your
working hours, 155–156
types of businesses suitable for,
156–158
using coaches for, 164–165
Time:
needed to cut down your
working hours, 155–156
not having enough, 108
people, systems, and tools to
free up, 17
use of free time, 146
Timebox, 138

TOB (*see* Team Operations Bible)
Tools, as pillar of business, 68–69
Top Five Regrets of the Dying
(Ware), 150
Training:
lack of expertise in, 82
as pillar of business, 75–76
Transactions:
increasing average size of,
131–132
per customer or per
salesperson, 132–134
Travel, evaluating your, 55, 57

VA (*see* Virtual assistant)
Vacations, evaluating your, 55, 57
Value proposition, 135–136
Victim mindset, 30
Virtual assistant (VA), 19–21,
86–90, 96
Virtual book camp, 145

Ware, Bronnie, 150
Weaknesses, understanding your,
30, 98
Wealth creation, 66
Wealth Dynamics assessment,
85, 98
Weekly goal trackers, 121
Weekly performance reviews, 122
What for technique, 148, 160
"What If" technique, 148–150
Working hours, 154–155
and earning more, 128
new projects requiring
adjustment in, 163
staying on track with, 159–160
time needed to cut down,
155–156
what to do in your, 162
Working smarter, 142, 165

ABOUT THE AUTHOR

Knolly Williams, the Business Healer, is a bestselling author, an international speaker, and a thought leader who runs three separate and distinct six-figure businesses while working just 3 Hours a Day. He teaches thousands of entrepreneurs and business leaders how to duplicate that success.

An entrepreneur for more than 40 years, Knolly has built multiple six- and seven-figure businesses from scratch. He built a seven-figure record label in his twenties. In his thirties, he became one of America's top real estate brokers, selling more than 1,000 homes as a solo agent during his first 10 years in real estate. In his forties, he was on the seminar circuit, speaking in more than 70 cities. Today, Knolly inspires tens of thousands through his YouTube channel, his Knolly Coaching Club, and his *3 Hours a Day Virtual Bootcamp*.

Today, Knolly Williams is recognized as the authority on how to quadruple your business while working just three hours per day. But life for Knolly wasn't always so grand. Childhood for Knolly was tough. He was born in Brooklyn, New York, in 1970, and soon his mom and dad moved the family to Dayton, Ohio. When Knolly was seven years old, his mom and dad separated. Knolly was deeply affected by the splitting of his family. When he was 10, Knolly's mom moved him and his sister, Felicia, to South Central Los Angeles.

From the time of his parents' separation, Knolly endured physical, emotional, and psychological abuse at the hands of his angry mother. He recalls waking up many a morning with painful, stinging welts from yet another extension cord beating. He was continually told that he was worthless and that his life would never amount to anything.

Knolly spent many of his summer vacations with his dad. At the age of 12, Knolly began his career in sales and marketing when he began helping his dad (Knolly, Sr.) sell his handcrafted jewelry at the local college and weekly flea markets. Soon, Knolly Jr.'s natural entrepreneurial habits kicked in and he started selling his own line of products ranging from candy to posters of his favorite singers.

When Knolly turned 16, he ran away from home and never looked back. He lived on the streets (from house to house) until the age of 18, when he was rescued by his uncle and moved to Austin, Texas. In Austin, Knolly discovered a world he never knew existed, one where he could thrive as an entrepreneur. At 21, he met the love of his life (Josefina) at church, and they married soon afterward.

At the age of 22, Knolly raised $1,800 in donations from friends and family and launched his first business, a gospel music magazine and Christian music record label. Within six years, his company was generating more than $150,000 per month, and he made his first $1 million by the time he was 29.

But despite his financial success, Knolly was working 14 to 16 hours each day and his life was way out of balance. Then, after 10 successful years, the music industry shifted from CDs to digital music. Knolly fell behind the trend and he and his wife had to walk away from everything, including their beautiful 6,000-square-foot home on 10 acres. Knolly hit rock bottom and had to start over.

Knolly obtained his real estate license and began selling real estate in Austin in 2004, and by 2008 he was the number one selling real estate agent in Austin, Texas (ranked by *Austin Business Journal* out of more than 9,800 agents and based on actual production).

Knolly listed and sold more than 1,000 houses during his first 10 years in the business, which placed him within the top 1 percent of real estate brokers in the United States. And Knolly achieved this success while working just three hours a day, taking nights and weekends off, going on four to five vacations a year, and being debt-free. He had cracked the code to working less while having and living more.

While the money was good and all the accolades helped build his wounded self-esteem, Knolly knew that the next chapter of his life was meant for something bigger. It was time to pay it forward and give back. Knolly wanted to share with other entrepreneurs and business leaders an easier way to success.

The most common mistake made by business leaders and entrepreneurs is measuring success against the hours put into their careers. Your success relies on your ability to systemize, organize, automate, and delegate tasks in order to stay OUT of the weeds and focus on growing your business. Knolly Williams, the Business Healer, has developed his methodology to get you to the ultimate goal: working just 3 Hours a Day, by focusing on only two Big Picture Priorities and delegating all else. As a leader, your value isn't in putting out small fires. It's in the inspiration and motivation of your team to operate at their peak potential.

In 2014, Knolly hit the speaking circuit, and over the years since, he has brought his life-changing seminars to thousands and spoken in over 100 cities.

Knolly knows what it's like to feel unloved, unworthy, and to lose everything. He believes that many entrepreneurs are trapped in the hustle and grind, and they don't see a way out. While the hustle is fun for a season, it is not meant for a lifetime.

Today, Knolly empowers business leaders and entrepreneurs to spark growth in their businesses by reconnecting to their passion and internal drives. His business healing method teaches you to systemize, organize, automate, and delegate your business in order to create freedom in your finances, time, and location.

The only way to get out of the weeds is to prioritize. Knolly has created a system that makes you focus on only the two top priorities and then a system to delegate everything else. By creating that two-priority system, you can create a three-hour workday and have a chance to truly focus on creating big value and financial freedom. It's a system to organize, automate, and delegate so you can focus on the drive and passion that will grow your business. With 3 Hours a Day, Knolly Williams has provided an actionable, step-by-step plan to untangle yourself from the weeds and free up your time in order to live and lead better.